Embracing Wabi-Sabi

Finding Beauty in Imperfection and Simplicity

Clara Yamamoto

© Copyright 2024 - All rights reserved.

The content contained within this book may not be reproduced, duplicated or transmitted without direct written permission from the author or the publisher.

Under no circumstances will any blame or legal responsibility be held against the publisher, or author, for any damages, reparation, or monetary loss due to the information contained within this book, either directly or indirectly.

Legal Notice:

This book is copyright protected. It is only for personal use. You cannot amend, distribute, sell, use, quote or paraphrase any part, or the content within this book, without the consent of the author or publisher.

Disclaimer Notice:

Please note the information contained within this document is for educational and entertainment purposes only. All effort has been executed to present accurate, up to date, reliable, complete information. No warranties of any kind are declared or implied. Readers acknowledge that the author is not engaging in the rendering of legal, financial, medical or professional advice. The content within this book has been derived from various sources. Please consult a licensed professional before attempting any techniques outlined in this book.

By reading this document, the reader agrees that under no circumstances is the author responsible for any losses, direct or indirect, that are incurred as a result of the use of information contained within this document, including, but not limited to, errors, omissions, or inaccuracies.

Table of Contents

INTRODUCTION

The book "Embracing Wabi-Sabi: Finding Beauty in Imperfection and Simplicity" offers an engaging look at the Japanese idea of Wabi-Sabi, which finds beauty in life's imperfect, fleeting, and incomplete parts. This book challenges readers to see things differently, to value the growth and decay cycle in nature, and to find comfort in impermanence and simplicity. The Wabi-Sabi philosophy encourages us to accept the imperfect and the incomplete in a world that is becoming more and more fixated on speedy consumption and perfection.

With its roots in Zen Buddhism and its influence on Japanese art, architecture, and everyday life, the book explores the historical and cultural beginnings of Wabi-Sabi. The author elucidates the application of this aesthetic to contemporary existence through evocative depictions and reflective analysis. Discovering how Wabi-Sabi may improve one's life in all spheres—from home décor to interpersonal interactions and personal development—is the path that readers are led through.

"Embracing Wabi-Sabi" is more than simply a philosophical manual; it's a helpful manual with doable advice for developing a Wabi-Sabi attitude. It offers activities, mindfulness techniques, and true-life tales that show how accepting simplicity and imperfection may result in a more contented and genuine life. Readers will have a stronger appreciation for life's inherent faults at the end of the book, having learned how to find beauty in the commonplace and the fleeting.

CHAPTER I

The Essence of Wabi-Sabi

Historical Origins

The Japanese aesthetic and philosophical idea of wabi-sabi has captured the imaginations and hearts of people who find beauty in imperfection and simplicity. Understanding Wabi-Sabi's historical roots, which are firmly anchored in Zen Buddhism and Japan's cultural development, is crucial to appreciating its enormous effect. This investigation shows how Wabi-Sabi has influenced Japanese daily life, art, and architecture while providing a counterbalance to Western standards of perfection and beauty.

It is thought that the ideas of Zen Buddhism, which emphasizes the fleeting nature of life and the value of awareness, are where the concept of Wabi-Sabi first emerged. The 12th century saw the introduction of Zen Buddhism to Japan, which brought with it an emphasis on austerity, simplicity, and respect for the natural world. The Japanese people found great resonance in these ideals and started incorporating them into their cultural customs. "Wabi-sabi" is a compound word made up of the terms "wabi" and "sabi." In the past, "sabi" denoted the beauty that comes with age, while "wabi" related to the isolation of living in the great outdoors, far from civilization. These meanings changed throughout time. Wabi is a term that may be used to describe both natural and artificial objects, and it originally denoted a rustic simplicity, freshness, or silence. On the other hand, sabi is the beauty or calm that comes with age, when wear and patina reveal the life and transience of the object.

One of the most important cultural activities that embodies Wabi-Sabi is the tea ceremony, or chanoyu. Sen no Rikyū, a tea master who is frequently credited with perfecting and popularizing Wabi-Sabi aesthetics, had a significant influence on the tea ceremony's formalization in the 16th century. Rikyū prioritized naturalness, simplicity, and humility in the tea ritual, favoring handcrafted, rustic tea bowls and utensils over ornate, polished ones. This change was a reflection of a deeper awareness of the temporary and the imperfect in culture. The purpose of the tea ceremony was to create an environment where people might appreciate the beauty of simplicity and the passing of time in addition to drinking tea. The tea bowl (chawan), tea scoop (chashaku), and tea whisk (chasen) are among the equipment used in the ceremony. These were frequently picked because of their rustic and flawed appearances. Beyond the tea ceremony, Rikyū's impact shaped Japanese aesthetics in a variety of art and design disciplines.

Wabi-Sabi is reflected in another cultural activity known as Ikebana, which is the Japanese art of flower arranging. Ikebana stresses naturalness, simplicity, and the beauty of imperfection, much like the tea ceremony. The natural shapes of the plants and the gaps between them are highlighted by arrangements that are frequently simple and asymmetrical. This method is in contrast to the more ornate and symmetrical floral arrangements associated with Western customs. In order to depict the fleeting essence of life and the beauty of impermanence, ikebana practitioners aim to achieve a sense of harmony between the arrangement and its surroundings. The use of faded leaves, branches that display scars, and flowers in different phases of bloom all highlight Wabi-Sabi's awareness of time and natural imperfection.

Wabi-sabi has influenced Japanese architecture as well. Wabi-Sabi concepts are frequently embodied in traditional Japanese dwellings, or Minka, through their use of natural materials, minimalist design, and interaction with the surrounding landscape. These houses usually have tatami mats, paper screens (shoji), and wooden beams that give them a cozy, homey feel. With its massive windows and sliding doors that open to gardens and let natural light flood the internal areas, the building stresses a connection to nature. The actual gardens are created with features like moss-covered stones, worn wooden bridges, and ponds with uneven shapes to give the impression of being natural and unmanicured. Residents are inspired to appreciate the beauty of the natural world and the passing of time by this aesthetic, which fosters a calm and reflective mood.

The impact of Wabi-Sabi can also be seen in Japanese ceramics and pottery. The deliberate flaws in the ceramics manufactured by Japanese potters demonstrate the aesthetic appreciation of the asymmetrical, handmade, and uneven. For instance, tea bowls made in the Raku pottery technique are prized for their distinctive glazes, asymmetrical designs, and rough textures. These objects are thought to represent the Wabi-Sabi appreciation of the imperfect and the fleeting, reflecting the hand of the potter and the organic firing process. The idea of impermanence and the beauty that comes with aging is further enhanced by the use of natural glazes that fracture and vary with time.

The development of Wabi-Sabi in Japanese culture is a reflection of a more significant social acceptance of imperfection and life's fleeting nature. This viewpoint permeates Japanese culture profoundly, impacting not only everyday behaviors and attitudes but also art and design. The Japanese technique of restoring shattered artifacts demonstrates acceptance of imperfection. Kintsugi, often known as "golden joinery," is the technique of using lacquer infused with powdered platinum, silver, or gold to mend shattered ceramics. Kintsugi draws attention to the damage rather than covering it up, making the object more exquisite and one-of-a-kind because of its past. The Wabi-Sabi philosophy, which holds that defects can add to an object's beauty rather than take away from it, is embodied in this technique.

The poetry and writing of Japan also embody the Wabi-Sabi concepts. Haiku is a classic kind of Japanese poetry that frequently depicts ephemeral moments of beauty in the natural world, symbolizing life's impermanence and transience. Haiku's simplicity and succinctness are in line with Wabi-Sabi aesthetics, condensing insightful insights into a small number of well-chosen words. Haiku frequently explores themes of impermanence, solitude, and the shifting of the seasons; this reflects Wabi-Sabi's appreciation of the fleeting beauty of the natural world.

Wabi-Sabi presents an alternative viewpoint to Western conceptions of beauty, which frequently place an emphasis on symmetry, stability, and perfection. It promotes an appreciation of the incomplete, imperfect, and fleeting. The manner in which Japanese society appreciates weathering and natural aging is a clear indication of this conceptual difference. In contrast to Western societies, which frequently work to maintain or return goods to their former state, Japanese culture typically embraces wear and tear, viewing these marks as a reflection of an object's past and personality.

The philosophical and cultural change towards an acceptance of imperfection and impermanence can be seen in the historical roots of Wabi-Sabi. Wabi-Sabi, which has its roots in Zen Buddhism and is shaped by Japanese cultural practices, has impacted many facets of Japanese daily life as well as art and design. It promotes a more thoughtful and appreciative view of the world by providing a counterbalance to Western standards of perfection and beauty. By adopting the Wabi-Sabi philosophy, one can develop a closer relationship with nature and the fleeting essence of life by finding beauty in the ordinary, the modest, and the imperfect.

In conclusion, a rich and complex aesthetic that has influenced Japanese society for generations may be seen in the historical roots of wabi-sabi. Wabi-Sabi ideas, which emphasize simplicity, naturalness, and the beauty of imperfection, have influenced many kinds of art and design, from the tea ceremony and Ikebana to architecture and ceramics. This philosophy offers a distinct viewpoint that contrasts with Western notions of beauty and perfection, encouraging an appreciation for the fleeting and incomplete. We can develop a stronger sense of awareness, contentment, and appreciation for the flawed beauty of the world around us by comprehending and loving Wabi-Sabi.

Origins in Zen Buddhism

Zen Buddhism is the source of Wabi-Sabi, a unique aesthetic and philosophical idea that originated in Japan. This relationship had a significant influence on the evolution of Wabi-Sabi, instilling in it a great respect for impermanence, imperfection, and simplicity. Examining the philosophical and historical development of Zen Buddhism, its introduction to Japan, and the ways in which its ideas influenced Japanese society and finally gave rise to Wabi-Sabi is necessary to comprehend this link.

One Mahayana branch of Buddhism called Zen places a strong emphasis on meditation and firsthand experience as a means of achieving nirvana. Zen Buddhism was brought to Japan in the 12th century after being introduced as Chan Buddhism in China under the Tang dynasty. The Zen tradition emphasizes awareness, appreciating the present moment, and practicing zazen, or seated meditation. Zen places a higher value on individual experience and the understanding that everything is interrelated than other Buddhist schools that could be more concerned with texts and rituals.

The samurai elite and the intellectuals welcomed Zen Buddhism when it came to Japan, and as a result, it had a profound impact on everyday life as well as art and architecture. Zen philosophy, which emphasizes austerity, simplicity, and naturalness, struck a profound chord with Japanese culture. These ideals stood in stark contrast to the previously commonplace, more complex, and intricate cultural activities. Zen's emphasis on life's impermanence and acceptance of imperfection laid the intellectual groundwork for the eventual development of the idea of Wabi-Sabi.

"Wabi-sabi" itself is a compound word that originated from the terms "wabi" and "sabi." Originally, "sabi" denoted the beauty that comes with age, encompassing the patina and wear of goods throughout time, while "wabi" related to the isolation and loneliness of living in the great outdoors, away from society. These phrases acquired new connotations when Zen Buddhism made an impact on Japanese culture. "Wabi" evolved to represent a peaceful, fresh, and rustic quality that could be ascribed to both naturally occurring and man-made artifacts. The term "sabi" came to mean the beauty or tranquility that appears with age, signifying the transience of things and their life.

Grasp Wabi-Sabi requires a grasp of Zen's teachings on impermanence, or "mujo," as they are known in Japanese. Nothing stays the same and everything is constantly changing, according to Zen Buddhism. This knowledge encourages acceptance of change and deterioration as well as a profound appreciation for the present. This translates into a style that honors the fleeting and transitory in the framework of Wabi-Sabi. Because they hold the markings of time and use, things that exhibit wear and age—like a cracked pottery bowl or an aged wooden beam—are viewed as more beautiful.

The creation of Wabi-Sabi is also significantly influenced by the Zen idea of "sunyata," or emptiness. According to Sunyata, nothing exists in a vacuum, and everything is interrelated. This idea promotes humility and an understanding of the limits of human perception. This translates to a Wabi-Sabi appreciation of the voids and spaces between things, of peaceful times, and of the subtle beauty of simplicity. It is a celebration of the things that go unspoken and are not immediately apparent.

The Japanese tea ceremony, known as chanoyu, is one of the most essential cultural customs that embodies Wabi-Sabi and is influenced by Zen Buddhism. Sen no Rikyū, a tea master who is frequently credited with perfecting and popularizing Wabi-Sabi aesthetics, had a significant influence on the tea ceremony's formalization in the 16th century. Rikyū prioritized naturalness, simplicity, and humility in the tea ritual, favoring handcrafted, rustic tea bowls and utensils over ornate, polished ones. This change was a reflection of a deeper awareness of the temporary and the imperfect in culture. The purpose of the tea ceremony was to create an environment where people might appreciate the beauty of simplicity and the passing of time in addition to drinking tea. The tea bowl (chawan), tea scoop (chashaku), and tea whisk (chasen) are among the equipment used in the ceremony. These were frequently picked because of their rustic and flawed appearances. Beyond the tea ceremony, Rikyū's impact shaped Japanese aesthetics in a variety of art and design disciplines.

Another example of how Zen Buddhism influenced Wabi-Sabi is the Japanese flower arrangement technique known as Ikebana. Ikebana stresses naturalness, simplicity, and the beauty of imperfection, much like the tea ceremony. The natural shapes of the plants and the gaps between them are highlighted by arrangements that are frequently simple and asymmetrical. This method is in contrast to the more ornate and symmetrical floral arrangements associated with Western customs. In order to depict the fleeting essence of life and the beauty of impermanence, ikebana practitioners aim to achieve a sense of harmony between the arrangement and its surroundings. The use of faded leaves, branches that display scars, and flowers in different phases of bloom all highlight Wabi-Sabi's awareness of time and natural imperfection.

Furthermore, the incorporation of Wabi-Sabi aesthetics is demonstrated by Zen's influence on Japanese pottery, namely the Raku pottery technique. Raku ceramics are prized for their distinctive glazes, asymmetrical shapes, and rough textures; they are utilized in tea ceremonies. These objects capture the essence of Wabi-Sabi, which values the fleeting and imperfect. They also show the potter's hand and the natural firing process. The idea of impermanence and the beauty that comes with aging is further enhanced by the use of natural glazes that fracture and vary with time.

Zen Buddhism has influenced Japanese architecture, as evidenced by the style of traditional houses and gardens. Wabi-sabi principles are reflected in the blending of indoor and outdoor spaces, the use of natural materials, and minimalist design. The warmth and simplicity of traditional Japanese dwellings, or Minka, are accentuated by the use of tatami mats, paper screens (shoji), and wooden beams. With its massive windows and sliding doors that open to gardens and let natural light flood the internal areas, the building stresses a connection to nature. The actual gardens are created with features like moss-covered stones, worn wooden bridges, and ponds with uneven shapes to give the impression of being natural and unmanicured. Residents are inspired to appreciate the beauty of the natural world and the passing of time by this aesthetic, which fosters a calm and reflective mood.

In summary, the roots of Wabi-Sabi are closely linked to Zen Buddhist teachings. The conceptual basis of Wabi-Sabi was laid by the Zen teachings on impermanence, emptiness, and simplicity. These ideas have influenced many facets of Japanese culture, including tea ceremonies, flower arrangements, ceramics, and architecture. This aesthetic offers a distinct viewpoint that contrasts with Western notions of beauty and perfection by praising the beauty of imperfection and the fleeting aspect of life. Understanding the Zen Buddhist origins of Wabi-Sabi allows us to recognize the significant philosophical and cultural changes that have influenced this particular Japanese aesthetic and promote a more aware and grateful way of looking at the world.

Evolution through Japanese culture and aesthetics

With its roots in Zen Buddhism, the idea of Wabi-Sabi has changed dramatically over centuries in Japanese culture and aesthetics. This development shows how philosophical ideas have been deeply incorporated into daily life, impacting Japanese art, architecture, design, and cultural behaviors. The evolution of Wabi-Sabi in Japanese culture shows how tradition and invention interact dynamically to create a distinct aesthetic that celebrates imperfection, simplicity, and the passing of time.

The foundation for the development of Wabi-Sabi was established in Japan by the early impact of Zen Buddhism. As Zen ideas spread throughout Japanese culture, they started to show themselves in a variety of creative and cultural manifestations. The tea ritual, or chanoyu, is one of the oldest and most significant examples of Wabi-Sabi. The tea ceremony embodied the Wabi-Sabi aesthetic, mainly when conducted under the direction of tea masters such as Sen no Rikyū. Rikyū's tea ceremony stressed the charm of naturalness and rustic simplicity. He eschewed the expensive and grandiose in favor of the modest and flawed tea utensils, choosing instead those that were homemade, uneven, and humble. This inclination was a reflection of a more significant cultural movement that valued Wabi-Sabi's fundamental principles of the natural and raw.

The Japanese flower-arranging technique known as Ikebana also serves as an example of how Wabi-Sabi has developed across Japanese society. Ikebana techniques have evolved to incorporate the ideas of asymmetry, minimalism, and organic beauty. Ikebana floral arrangements are purposefully sparse and asymmetrical, emphasizing the natural forms of the plants and the spaces between them, in contrast to Western floral arrangements that frequently strive for symmetrical perfection. This method emphasizes a core Wabi-Sabi understanding of the imperfect and the fleeting. Ikebana's beauty is found in its capacity to capture the essence of nature, with all of its imperfections and transience, rather than in its perfection.

Japanese ceramics and pottery provide more evidence of the Wabi-Sabi's cultural development. Wabi-Sabi aesthetics are particularly embodied in the Raku ceramic tradition. Raku porcelain is distinguished by its distinctive glazes, asymmetrical shapes, and rough textures; it is utilized in tea ceremonies. These ceramic works are prized for their uniqueness and the artist's hand marks rather than their symmetry or perfection. Raku pottery is made with a lot of spontaneity and acceptance of uncertainty, which reflects the Wabi-Sabi aesthetic that values imperfection and the beauty of the unintentional. These ideas were eventually adopted by other Japanese ceramic traditions, such as Bizen and Shigaraki ware, which produced objects that emphasized earthy hues, natural textures, and the special effects of kiln fire.

Traditional Japanese houses and gardens have been designed and built with the concepts of Wabi-Sabi in mind. Bamboo, paper, and wood are common natural materials found in traditional Japanese dwellings or minka. These materials were picked because they will age beautifully and gain a patina over time, adding to rather than taking away from their beauty. These homes' designs place a strong emphasis on practicality, simplicity, and a harmonious relationship with the surrounding landscape. Shoji and fusuma, or large sliding doors and paper screens, provide flexible use of space and blur the line between indoor and outdoor areas. With features like worn wooden structures, ponds with irregular shapes, and stones covered in moss, gardens are intended to look natural and unmanicured. This design inspires people to appreciate the beauty of imperfection and the passing of time by fostering a calm and reflective atmosphere.

The literary and poetic works of Japan also demonstrate the cultural development of Wabi-Sabi. Haiku is a classic kind of Japanese poetry that depicts the ephemeral and transitory aspects of life by capturing brief moments of beauty in the natural world. Haiku's simplicity and succinctness are in line with Wabi-Sabi aesthetics, condensing insightful insights into a small number of well-chosen words. Haiku frequently explores themes of impermanence, solitude, and the shifting of the seasons; this reflects Wabi-Sabi's appreciation of the fleeting beauty of the natural world. These ideas are also present in classic Japanese literature, such as Matsuo Bashō's works, which express profound philosophical ideas using sparse, evocative language.

The Japanese visual arts, such as calligraphy and painting, are influenced by Wabi-Sabi. The use of straightforward brushstrokes and a focus on negative space in Sumi-e, or ink-wash painting, reflects the aesthetics of Wabi-Sabi. Sumi-e paintings frequently use sparse detail to capture the spirit of natural situations, aiming for essence over exact realism. This method is in line with the Wabi-Sabi aesthetic, which values imperfection, simplicity, and the beauty of the incomplete. Similar to this, each brushstroke's spontaneity and uniqueness are valued in Japanese calligraphy or shodo. The fluidity and distinct expression of the artist's hand in calligraphy, which embraces flaws and differences as part of its allure, are what make it so beautiful.

Wabi-Sabi is still relevant today, influencing both modern lifestyle and design. Wabi-sabi principles and the minimalist design movement are similar in many ways. The minimalist movement emphasizes functionality, simplicity, and a reduction of excess. Wabi-Sabi is a popular source of inspiration for modern architects and designers, who use natural materials, subdued color schemes, and an emphasis on the inherent beauty of imperfection in their designs. A Wabi-Sabi admiration for the one-of-a-kind and flawed is also reflected in the popularity of handcrafted and artisanal goods. Wabi-Sabi provides a counterbalance to a society that is becoming more and more controlled by mass production and digital perfection by valuing individuality, authenticity, and the passage of time.

The Wabi-Sabi ideology has also found resonance in the larger global environment, impacting lifestyle and mindfulness practices in addition to design and art. The emphasis on being aware and practicing sustainable living is in line with current tendencies towards living simply, appreciating the present, and finding beauty in the imperfect. Wabi-Sabi promotes a slower, more deliberate way of living that strengthens one's bond with nature and heightens one's awareness of the fleeting, little moments that make up each day.

In summary, the development of Wabi-Sabi via Japanese aesthetics and society illustrates a deep integration of philosophical ideas with daily existence. The tea ceremony and Ikebana, as well as ceramics, architecture, literature, and visual arts, have all contributed to the development of Wabi-Sabi, a distinct aesthetic that honors imperfection, simplicity, and the passing of time. This development shows how innovation and tradition interact dynamically to create a cultural legacy that still influences and resonates with modern design and lifestyle choices. By adopting the Wabi-Sabi philosophy, we can develop a greater appreciation for the beauty that lies in the flawed and fleeting, discovering significance and depth in the ordinary things in life.

Philosophical Foundations

The philosophical underpinnings of Wabi-Sabi, a deeply rooted aesthetic and worldview in Japanese society, are complex and multidimensional, mainly derived from traditional Japanese beliefs and Zen Buddhism. This foundational philosophy highlights the impermanence of life, the beauty of imperfection, and a deep appreciation for simplicity. Gaining knowledge of these philosophical foundations helps us understand how Wabi-Sabi influences our perceptions of beauty, life, and the outside world.

Wabi-Sabi is centered around the idea of impermanence, or "mujo," as it is known in Japanese. Zen Buddhism, which maintains that nothing stays the same and that everything is constantly changing, is the primary source of inspiration for this concept. A profound appreciation of the present moment and an acceptance of the natural cycle of birth, growth, decay, and death are fostered by this awareness of impermanence. Impermanence in the context of Wabi-Sabi corresponds to an aesthetic that emphasizes the fleeting and the ephemeral. Because they represent time passing and the inevitable process of change, transient things and experiences that exhibit wear and age are deemed lovely. This viewpoint promotes an awareness of beauty's transient nature and an appreciation of the present.

Accepting imperfections is one of the core tenets of Wabi-Sabi. Whereas Western standards tend to emphasize symmetry, perfection, and permanence, Wabi-Sabi celebrates imperfection, irregularity, and incompleteness as sources of beauty. The Zen idea of "wabi," which initially alluded to the isolation and melancholy of living in nature, away from society, is strongly linked to this awareness of imperfection. "Wabi" eventually came to represent a modest elegance and rustic simplicity. This change in meaning is indicative of a more extensive acceptance of the flawed and the lowly in society. The premise is that genuine beauty can be found in the authenticity and character that come with imperfection, not in perfection.

Another fundamental component of Wabi-Sabi is the idea of "sunyata," or emptiness, from Zen Buddhism. According to Sunyata, nothing exists in a vacuum, and everything is interrelated. This knowledge promotes humility and an awareness of the limitations of human perspective. This translates to a Wabi-Sabi appreciation of the voids and spaces between things, of peaceful times, and of the subtle beauty of simplicity. It values the subtle and nuanced over the overt and the obvious, and it praises what is not expressed or instantly apparent. This idea promotes a minimalist aesthetic in which the absence of features enhances the beauty of an object or setting, emphasizing the idea that less is more.

The traditional Japanese appreciation of nature and natural materials also informs Wabi-Sabi. The use of raw, natural materials in Japanese buildings, designs, and art is indicative of this. Because they patina and age gracefully, materials like clay, stone, wood, and bamboo are preferred. Rather than being viewed as defects, age, wear, and weathering are additions that give an object more dimension and personality. This admiration for organic materials and methods is a reflection of the larger Wabi-Sabi philosophy, which honors the simple and the natural. It promotes a profound relationship with nature and an awareness of how humans fit into it.

The development of a contemplative lifestyle and the practice of mindfulness are two other ways that Zen Buddhism has influenced Wabi-Sabi. Zen philosophy places a strong emphasis on living in the present moment and facing life head-on, free from distraction or judgment. Wabi-Sabi, which promotes a close connection with the outside world and an appreciation for the small, often-overlooked moments in life, is centered around this thoughtful approach. By encouraging a sense of satisfaction and tranquility, mindfulness practice helps to develop an awareness of the beauty that may be found in the commonplace and ordinary.

Wabi-Sabi is influenced by traditional Japanese aesthetics and cultural practices in addition to its Zen Buddhist foundations. One of the best examples of how Wabi-Sabi concepts are incorporated into cultural traditions is the Japanese tea ceremony or chanoyu. The principles of simplicity, humility, and the beauty of imperfection are highlighted in the tea ceremony, especially as they are perfected by tea master Sen no Rikyū. The tea bowl (Dhawan) and tea scoop (chashaku), two tools used in the ceremony, are frequently handmade and selected for their rustic, uneven characteristics. This selection honors the imperfections that give each piece character and shows the Wabi-Sabi appreciation for items that bear the signs of their production and use.

Wabi-Sabi is also embodied in the Japanese art of flower arranging, ikebana. The natural shapes of the plants and the gaps between them are highlighted in ikebana arrangements, which are frequently simple and asymmetrical. This method highlights the Wabi-Sabi admiration for simplicity and naturalness and contrasts with more ornate and symmetrical floral arrangements found in the West. The use of faded leaves, branches with scars, and blooming flowers at different times all highlight the beauty of imperfection and the fleeting essence of life.

Japanese ceramics and pottery provide additional examples of the Wabi-Sabi philosophy. Raku pottery, for instance, is distinguished by its irregular shapes, rough textures, and distinctive glazes. These pieces are prized for their uniqueness and the artist's handiwork, not for their symmetry or perfection. Raku pottery is made with a lot of spontaneity and acceptance of uncertainty, which reflects the Wabi-Sabi aesthetic that values imperfection and the beauty of the unintentional. A fundamental component of Wabi-Sabi is its respect for the imperfect and the unique, which promotes acceptance of the raw and unpolished.

Wabi-sabi principles can be found in the themes of impermanence, simplicity, and the beauty of the commonplace in Japanese literature and poetry. Haiku is a classic form of Japanese poetry that condenses deep thoughts into a few well-chosen words, capturing ephemeral moments of beauty in nature. Haiku's simplicity and brevity are in line with Wabi-Sabi aesthetics, which emphasize the fleeting essence of life and the significance of the present. Classical Japanese literature, like the works of Matsuo Bashō, exemplifies these ideals as well, communicating profound philosophical concepts using sparse and atmospheric language.

Wabi-Sabi's philosophical underpinnings are still relevant in today's design and lifestyle trends. Wabi-sabi principles and the minimalist design movement are similar in many ways. The minimalist movement emphasizes functionality, simplicity, and a reduction of excess. Wabi-Sabi is a popular source of inspiration for modern architects and designers, who use natural materials, subdued color schemes, and an emphasis on the inherent beauty of imperfection in their designs. The appeal of artisanal and handcrafted products also reflects a Wabi-Sabi appreciation of the one-of-a-kind and flawed, honoring the maker's markings and the distinctive qualities of every item.

Wabi-Sabi, in summary, has philosophical roots in Zen Buddhism and ancient Japanese beliefs. It emphasizes the impermanence of existence, the beauty of imperfection, and a strong appreciation for simplicity. These ideas create a distinct aesthetic that honors the fleeting, the subtle, and the natural, promoting mindfulness and gratitude in daily life. We can develop a closer relationship with the world around us and discover beauty and purpose in the ordinary, imperfect moments that make up our daily lives by adopting Wabi-Sabi. This way of thinking encourages us to find richness and depth in the natural cycles of growth and decay as well as in the modest, unpretentious parts of life, providing a counterbalance to the search for perfection and permanence.

Comparison with Western philosophies

Many Western conceptions of beauty, existence, and art stand in stark contrast to the Japanese aesthetics and culture of Wabi-Sabi. Wabi-Sabi offers an alternative worldview that departs significantly from Western ideas of beauty, permanence, and symmetry by emphasizing imperfection, transience, and simplicity. In addition to highlighting Wabi-Sabi's distinctive features, analyzing these variations sheds light on the more significant philosophical and cultural divide between the East and the West.

The emphasis placed by Wabi-Sabi on imperfection stands in stark contrast to the Western approach, which has its roots in classical Greek philosophy, which is to pursue perfect forms and beauty. Western aesthetics has been impacted by the ideas of ancient Greek philosophers like Plato and Aristotle for millennia, who proposed that harmony, proportion, and symmetry are the fundamental components of beauty. According to Plato's theory of forms, the material world is merely an imperfect representation of a more perfect reality. This concept permeates Western architecture and art, which frequently aim for flawless forms and idealized portrayals. Wabi-Sabi, on the other hand, finds beauty in the unfinished, erratic, and imperfect. It celebrates the individuality and character that imperfections give to things and places, valuing the signs of usage and time.

A further significant influence on Western aesthetics has come from the Enlightenment and the advent of rationalism, which placed a strong emphasis on reason, control, and order. The Enlightenment promoted the ideas of progress, human perfection, and the ability to rationally reshape the world. The symmetry of Renaissance art, the planned gardens of European palaces, and the accuracy and consistency of Western classical music are examples of this worldview in action. On the other hand, Wabi-Sabi emphasizes an organic order that results from accepting things as they are and celebrates the natural and the spontaneous. The tendency in the West to force human will and order upon the natural world contrasts with this acceptance of unpredictable and natural processes.

Wabi-Sabi's appreciation of transience and ephemerality contrasts with the Western emphasis on permanence and durability. Western philosophy and religion frequently aim for eternal truths or immortal legacies, transcending the transitory realm. For instance, Christianity's focus on the everlasting soul and eternal life has an impact on Western perceptions of permanence in art and architecture. This goal for durability and permanence is reflected in the enormous architecture, impressive sculptures, and robust materials. Inspired by Zen Buddhism, Wabi-Sabi acknowledges and values life's transience. It sees beauty in things that pass quickly and are transient, like cherry blossoms that fall or the worn patina of old wood. This viewpoint promotes an awareness of the fleeting aspect of life and a thoughtful interaction with the present.

The foundation of Wabi-Sabi, the Zen Buddhist concept of "sunyata," or emptiness, also offers a philosophical departure from Western ideas. According to Sunyata, everything is interrelated, and emptiness is a necessary component of life. This idea fosters an appreciation for the voids between things, the quiet in between noises, and the invisible facets of existence. Western philosophies frequently stress individualism and the distinction between things and beings, particularly those that are influenced by Cartesian dualism. The well-known aphorism "Cogito, ergo sum" (I think, therefore I am) by René Descartes emphasizes the idea of personal existence and independence. On the other hand, Wabi-Sabi highlights the interdependence of all things and relational existence as seen through the sunyata lens. This way of looking at things encourages modesty and a sense of balance with the larger scheme of things.

The Wabi-Sabi method of learning and understanding is in contrast to the Western desire for knowledge and dominance over nature. A worldview focused on the discovery, control, and enhancement of the natural environment has been fostered in the West by the scientific revolution and the ensuing technological achievements. This passion has produced outstanding results, but it has also fostered a dominance and resource-exploitation mentality. Wabi-Sabi promotes a considerate and long-lasting relationship with the environment since it is based on a more harmonious relationship with nature. It imparts the insight that comes from watching natural processes and the idea that attunement, not control, is the source of profound understanding. This way of thinking promotes sustainability, living in harmony with the environment, and understanding the boundaries of human interference.

Wabi-Sabi's acceptance of imperfection contrasts with Western notions of artistic excellence and the artist's position in the field of creativity. In Western tradition, the artist is frequently viewed as a creator who strives for a flawless final result and instills order and beauty into chaos. The "Renaissance man"—a Renaissance ideal— embodies the idea of the artist as a multi-talented artist who aspires to produce works of flawless and timeless beauty. Contrarily, Wabi-Sabi sees the artist as a partner with nature, with the creative process being just as significant as the finished work. This concept, which values spontaneity, natural materials, and the acceptance of accidental outcomes, is embodied in Japanese arts such as Ikebana, pottery, and tea ceremonies. The finished pieces are prized for their individuality and the obvious signs of the artist's hand; they exhibit a flawed and dynamic beauty.

Wabi-Sabi and Western philosophy differ philosophically in areas such as values and lifestyle. Western societies frequently place a strong emphasis on accomplishment, accumulation, and external success—especially those affected by the Protestant work ethic. This way of thinking encourages a society that values hard work, production, and material prosperity. On the other hand, Wabi-Sabi promotes minimalism, simplicity, and happiness with less. It promotes an everyday and daily existence that finds fulfillment in the ordinary, placing a higher priority on the intrinsic than the extrinsic. In contrast to the Western quest for advancement and perfection, this strategy promotes feelings of happiness and tranquility.

Finally, the comparison of Western and Wabi-Sabi philosophy reveals significant distinctions in the ways that existence, beauty, and art are viewed and appreciated. Western ideas of perfection, permanence, and logical order are challenged by Wabi-Sabi's acceptance of imperfection, transience, and simplicity. These opposing ideologies are a reflection of more enormous cultural divides, forming unique perspectives on life, art, and the natural world. We can better appreciate the diversity and depth of human thought as well as the ways that cultural viewpoints influence our experiences and interactions with the outside world by investigating and appreciating these variances. A thoughtful, modest, and harmonious style of living is encouraged by the Wabi-Sabi concept, which has the power to improve our lives and increase our awareness of the beauty inherent in the temporary and flawed.

Influence on Japanese art and daily life

An interesting topic that explores Japan's rich cultural past and its capacity to adapt and change due to a variety of internal and external forces is the effect on Japanese art and daily life. Japanese culture and daily life have had a profound impact on and have been influenced by the art form known for its distinct aesthetic and deep symbolism. This section examines the social, cultural, and historical factors that have influenced Japanese art and daily life, emphasizing significant eras and movements that have had a lasting impact on Japanese culture.

Japanese art has a rich and ancient history that stretches back to the Paleolithic era. Jomon pottery, with its elaborate motifs and patterns, is among the oldest types of Japanese art. The "cord-marked" ceramics from this era give rise to the moniker, which symbolizes the early Japanese people's ties to the natural world. Japan's artistic expressions started to take on new forms when it entered the Yayoi period. More intricate ceramic and bronze artwork resulted from the profound social and cultural shifts brought about by the arrival of rice farming from the Asian continent.

During the Asuka and Nara periods (538-794 AD), China and Korea had a powerful influence on Japanese art and daily life. Japanese culture was significantly impacted by the advent of Buddhism from China around the middle of the sixth century. Buddhist art became a significant form of artistic expression in Japan and was typified by sculptures, paintings, and temple architecture. A couple of the best instances of this influence are the Great Buddha of Nara and the Todai-ji Temple. Further enhancing Japanese culture was the incorporation of Chinese letters, or kanji, into the writing system, which made it easier to record historical events, religious texts, and poetry.

Even while Chinese influence persisted, Japan started to forge its own unique cultural identity during the Heian period (794–1185 AD). Famous Japanese literary and artistic works are a result of the Heian aristocracy's courtly culture. One of the world's first books, "The Tale of Genji" by Murasaki Shikibu, is regarded as a masterpiece of Japanese literature. During this time, Yamato-e, a genre of Japanese art that features scenes from mythology, literature, and history, also began to take shape. The vivid colors and deft brushwork of these pieces of art frequently reflected the sophisticated tastes of the Heian court.

Due to the introduction of new cultural and creative influences by the samurai class, Japanese art and daily life underwent a tremendous change during the Kamakura period (1185–1333 AD). The emphasis on realism and dynamic movement in the art of the time reflected the fighting mentality of the samurai. During this period, Zen Buddhism developed, which had a significant influence on Japanese aesthetics as well. The Zen concepts of peace, simplicity, and awareness were reflected in a variety of artistic mediums, such as tea ceremony (chanoyu), ink painting (sumi-e), and landscape design. Everlasting instances of this impact include the Zen temples' simple construction and Ryoan-ji's rock gardens.

With further development of Zen-influenced art forms, the Muromachi period (1336–1573) carried on the Kamakura period's traditions. In particular, the tea ceremony evolved into a highly ritualized practice that embodied the awareness of imperfection and transience, or wabi-sabi, which is a Zen concept. During this time, the flower-arranging technique known as ikebana emerged, highlighting the balance between human creativity and the natural world. With its thoughtfully placed stones, plants, and water elements, the Japanese tea garden has become an essential aspect of Japanese daily life and culture.

Azuchi-Momoyama (1573–1603 AD) was a period of thriving culture and political union. Throughout this time, strong daimyo (feudal rulers) built magnificent castles and lavished art and architecture on their subjects. Momoyama's paintings, with their vibrant hues and lively compositions, captured the grandeur and aspirations of the time. In Japanese homes and castles, sliding doors (fusuma) and folding screens (byobu) with colorful paintings became standard fixtures.

Under the Tokugawa shogunate, a protracted period of peace and stability was ushered in during the Edo period (1603–1868 AD). Because of this stability, a thriving urban culture grew, especially in Edo (now Tokyo), Kyoto, and Osaka. Known for its thriving popular culture, this era also saw the rise of ukiyo-e or woodblock prints that portrayed scenes of famous actors, landscapes, and urban life. Japanese art is still defined by the iconic pictures produced by artists such as Hokusai and Hiroshige. Outside of Japan, ukiyo-e influenced European artists of the 19th century's Japonisme movement, including Claude Monet and Vincent van Gogh.

The swift modernization and Westernization of Japan commenced with the Meiji Restoration of 1868. Western concepts and technologies have a significant influence on everyday life and art in Japan. Western techniques were frequently combined with traditional art traditions to create a distinctive mix of styles. The creation of organizations and art schools like the Tokyo School of Fine Arts made it easier for new artistic expressions to emerge. The adoption of Western dress, architecture, and technology has had a profound impact on Japanese daily life.

Japan has preserved a great regard for its traditional arts and cultural activities despite its fast industrialization.

Japanese art continued to develop in the 20th century, with movements like Nihonga (painting in the Japanese manner) and Sosaku Hanga (creative prints) highlighting the value of maintaining and advancing the past. Modern Japanese artists that combine traditional and contemporary elements in their works, like Yayoi Kusama and Takashi Murakami, have won praise from all over the world.

Japanese cultural traditions have a significant impact on daily living in addition to art. In contemporary Japan, traditional arts like calligraphy, ikebana, and tea ceremony are still practiced and appreciated. These exercises highlight principles that are important to Japanese culture, such as discipline, awareness, and a strong bond with the natural world. A sense of continuity and connection is created by festivals, customs, and seasonal events like the yearly Obon festival and hanami cherry blossom viewing, which link modern Japanese society to its ancient roots.

In conclusion, a complex interaction of historical, cultural, and social aspects has an influence on Japanese art and daily life. Japanese art has undergone several stages of development from the early Jomon era to the present, each of which has left a unique imprint on the country's cultural landscape. Traditional customs still have an impact on Japanese culture today, but foreign influences like Buddhism and Westernization have been included to enhance Japanese art. This complex and dynamic interaction between art and everyday life illustrates how resilient and flexible Japanese culture is, guaranteeing its continued influence and applicability in the contemporary era.

CHAPTER II

Wabi-Sabi in Art and Design

Traditional Japanese Art Forms

Japan's distinct aesthetic sensibility and rich cultural legacy are demonstrated by the country's traditional art genres. These centuries-old art forms include painting, ceramics, sculpture, performance arts, and crafts, among many other fields. The complex interaction that exists between the Japanese people and their surroundings is reflected in each art form, which contains particular cultural values, beliefs, and techniques. This section examines some of the most essential traditional Japanese art forms, emphasizing their artistic value, unique qualities, and historical evolution.

Pottery dates back to the Jomon period (c. 14,000 – 300 BCE), making it one of the oldest and most lasting forms of traditional Japanese art. The distinctive cord-marked designs found on Jomon ceramics were made by pressing cords into the clay prior to burning. Although the primary purposes of these ancient ceramics were cooking and storage, their elaborate designs also demonstrated an early sense of aesthetic beauty. As a result of contact with the Asian continent, new pottery techniques and styles were introduced during the Yayoi period (300 BCE–300 CE). In contrast to Jomon pottery, Yayoi pottery is distinguished by its smooth surfaces and more straightforward, elegant forms.

Significant advancements in Japanese art occurred throughout the Asuka and Nara periods (538–794), especially with the arrival of Buddhism from China and Korea. Buddhism influenced many artistic mediums, including sculpture, painting, and architecture, and it eventually formed a significant part of Japanese culture. The Great Buddha of Nara and other colossal Buddhist statues are examples of the significant influence of Buddhism on Japanese sculpture. These elaborately carved and gilded statues, which were frequently composed of wood or bronze, demonstrated both creative talent and religious devotion. Buddhist temple architecture, with its opulent constructions and ornate embellishments, also rose to prominence during this time.

The flourishing of courtly arts and literature made the Heian period (794–1185 CE) widely recognized as the pinnacle of classical Japanese civilization. During this period, the distinctive Japanese painting style known as Yamato-e evolved. In contrast to earlier works that drew extensively on Chinese techniques, Yamato-e paintings concentrated on Japanese topics, portraying events from mythology, history, and literature. The delicate brushwork, vivid colors, and minute details that defined these paintings. Emakimono, or illustrated handscrolls, which combined text and images to convey stories, were also created during the Heian period. One of the most well-known instances of this art style is the "Tale of Genji" scrolls, which are based on the famous novel by Murasaki Shikibu.

The samurai class rose to prominence during the Kamakura era (1185–1333 CE), which also saw a change in societal and aesthetic tastes. Realistic and dynamic movement were valued, and the samurai warrior culture was portrayed in this era's art. The invention of ink painting, or sumi-e, a monochromatic art technique that used various shades of black ink to produce expressive and evocative images, was one noteworthy advancement. Sumi-e, which was influenced by Zen Buddhism, placed a strong emphasis on spontaneity, simplicity, and the artist's spiritual connection to nature. During the Kamakura period, many Zen temples were built, which are distinguished by their calm rock gardens and simple architecture.

The Kamakura period's traditions were maintained during the Muromachi period (1336–1573), which saw the expansion of Zen-influenced art styles. During this period, the elaborate ritual known as the tea ceremony (chanoyu), which honors the making and drinking of matcha (powdered green tea), evolved into a highly sophisticated activity. The tea ceremony is a manifestation of wabi-sabi, a Zen concept that recognizes the beauty in impermanence and imperfection. Tea bowls and kettles, among other equipment used in the tea ceremony, were frequently made by talented artists by hand and reflected both practical and decorative aspects. During the Muromachi period, ikebana—a flower arrangement technique that emphasizes harmony, balance, and the inherent beauty of flowers—also rose to popularity.

During the Momoyama period (1573-1603 CE), powerful daimyo (feudal lords) built magnificent castles and lavishly supported art and architecture, resulting in a period of political union and cultural development. Momoyama's paintings, with their vibrant hues and lively compositions, captured the grandeur and aspirations of the time. In Japanese homes and castles, sliding doors (fusuma) and folding screens (byobu) with colorful paintings became standard fixtures. These pieces of art demonstrated the artists' command of both technique and narrative, frequently portraying historical events, natural landscapes, and mythological stories.

Traditional Japanese performing arts have contributed significantly to the nation's cultural legacy in addition to the visual arts. Noh theater, a traditional kind of Japanese theater that dates back to the fourteenth century, tells stories from literature, mythology, and history through a combination of dance, music, and drama. Slow, methodical motions, a simple stage design, and the usage of masks to represent many characters are characteristics of noh performances. Another classic Japanese theatrical style, kabuki, appeared in the early 17th century and is renowned for its dramatic makeup, intricate costumes, and dynamic performance. The tremendous theatrical traditions of Japan are being preserved through the performance of both noh and kabuki today.

To sum up, traditional Japanese art forms cover a broad spectrum of artistic disciplines, each with distinctive qualities and cultural value of its own. Japanese art styles represent the changing preferences, values, and philosophies of the country, from the exquisite ceramics of the Jomon period to the sophisticated paintings of the Heian period and from the dynamic ink paintings of the Kamakura period to the vivid woodblock prints of the Edo period. The fact that these traditional arts are still practiced and valued in contemporary Japan attests to the lasting influence of the nation's cultural inheritance and guarantees the survival of these artistic expressions as essential components of Japanese identity.

Tea ceremonies and tea ware

A pillar of Japanese culture, the tea ceremony—also referred to as chanoyu, sado, or chado in Japanese—embodies a blend of aesthetics, philosophy, and social activity. The tea ceremony, which has its roots in Zen Buddhism, is a complex ritual that honors attention, simplicity, and the beauty of the fleeting and flawed. It goes much beyond simply sipping tea. This section examines the origins of the tea ceremony, the elaborate choreography involved in its performance, and the importance and range of tea utensils utilized.

The arrival of tea from China during the Nara period (710-794 CE) is when the Japanese tea ritual first emerged. Tea was prized for its therapeutic qualities and capacity to facilitate meditation when it was first drunk, mainly by the affluent and Buddhist monks. Zen Buddhism had started to spread throughout Japan by the Kamakura period (1185–1333 CE), bringing with it the meditation techniques that would eventually shape the evolution of the tea ceremony. The tea ceremony took on its unique shape during the Muromachi period (1336–1573), partly as a result of the influence of tea masters like Murata Juko, who highlighted the intellectual and spiritual components of tea consumption.

Sen no Rikyu (1522-1591) is regarded as the most critical person in the history of the tea ceremony since he refined and formalized the custom. Tea ceremonies are based on the wabi-sabi philosophy of Rikyu, which recognizes beauty in imperfection, simplicity, and transience. His focus on the spiritual bond between host and guest, as well as on rustic simplicity, elevated the tea ceremony to an art form that went beyond simple hospitality. Tea room architecture, tea ware selection, and the painstaking choreography of the tea preparation process are all clearly influenced by Rikyu.

A chassis, or mainly designed tearoom or tea house, is the setting for a typical tea ceremony. The tearoom is a calm, minimalist area that is frequently built with organic materials like paper, bamboo, and wood. The tea room's entrance is purposefully low, encouraging visitors to approach with humility. The interior is adorned simply, with the focal point being a single scroll or a straightforward arrangement of flowers in the tokonoma (alcove), which serves as the ceremony's focal point. The tea room's simple design embodies the Zen idea of turning away distractions in order to cultivate concentration.

The actual tea ceremony is a highly ritualized procedure that is broken down into multiple phases, such as setting up the tearoom, welcoming guests, offering kaiseki, or light meals, and preparing and pouring tea. The person in charge of hosting the ceremony, known as the teishu, carefully plans out the tea room's layout and chooses the proper tools to create a peaceful mood. In response, the attendees approach the ceremony with a sense of reverence and focus, enjoying the calm and the small nuances of the occasion.

Matcha (powdered green tea) preparation and serving lie at the center of the tea ritual. The host employs a collection of specialty cutlery, each with a unique meaning and background. The act of serving and receiving tea establishes a direct line of communication between the host and visitor, making the chawan (tea bowl) possibly the most significant piece of teaware. Chawans differ widely in size, form, and style; some are earthy and rustic, while others are sophisticated and gorgeous. The chasen, also known as a tea whisk, is usually constructed from a single piece of bamboo and is used to whisk matcha into a frothy consistency. Matcha is kept in storage in a natsume or chaire (tea caddy), while the chashaku (tea scoop) is used to measure the tea powder.

Every tea set is thoughtfully chosen to fit the host's aesthetic tastes, the ceremony's theme, and the current season. The host's style and sensibility are reflected in the teaware selection, which frequently includes heirlooms that have been passed down through the generations to give the ceremony a feeling of continuity and history. Additionally, the teaware selections complement the other components of the tearoom, resulting in a harmonious and peaceful setting.

The admiration of tea ware revolves around the idea of wabi-sabi. This style places an emphasis on the patina of antiquity, asymmetrical designs, and the beauty of natural materials. For instance, a lot of highly valued chawan feature minor flaws and asymmetry that emphasize their handmade quality. These objects' history and use are marked by wear and tear, which adds to their worth and beauty rather than being perceived as defects. The higher spiritual ideals that underpin the tea ceremony are reflected in this appreciation of the imperfect and the fleeting.

The tea ceremony is a profoundly present and focused activity that extends beyond its physical components. In order to create a shared experience that goes beyond the ordinary, the host and the guests participate in the ritual with complete awareness of the present moment. A contemplative state that promotes a deeper connection with oneself and with others is fostered by the host's precise movements, the guests' silent contemplation, and the tranquil atmosphere of the tearoom.

In addition, the tea ceremony promotes respect and community through social rituals. Etiquette dictates how a host and visitor should interact, with a focus on respect, humility, and thankfulness. While the host shows concern and care for the visitors' comfort and experience, guests express gratitude for the host's efforts and the tea set utilized. The philosophy of the tea ceremony is centered on this idea of harmony and oneness, which is created via mutual respect and admiration.

The tea ceremony is still observed and valued in modern Japan as a way to cultivate oneself as well as a cultural tradition. Tea schools, like the Urasenke, Omotesenke, and Mushakojisenke, continue Sen no Rikyu's teachings by instructing students of all ages in the art of the tea ceremony. As a reflection of the interdependence of Japanese aesthetic traditions, the ideas of the tea ceremony also have an impact on other facets of Japanese culture, including calligraphy, garden design, and ikebana, or the arrangement of flowers.

To sum up, the Japanese tea ceremony is an elaborate and multidimensional art form with a complex philosophical background, elaborate procedures, and a long history. The tea ceremony provides a counterbalance to the complexity and diversions of modern life with its emphasis on awareness, simplicity, and the acceptance of imperfection. The tea ceremony cultivates a sense of harmony, presence, and connection that goes beyond the act of drinking tea. It accomplishes this through the thoughtful selection and usage of tea equipment, the establishment of a calm atmosphere, and the contemplative activity of making and serving tea. The tea ceremony is a living tradition that, through its ageless teachings and customs, never stops inspiring and improving the lives of those who participate.

Characteristics of Wabi-Sabi homes

The Japanese aesthetic concept of wabi-sabi, which honors simplicity, impermanence, and imperfection, is ingrained in Japanese society. Wabi-sabi, which has its roots in Zen Buddhism, places a strong emphasis on impermanence, acceptance, modesty, and natural processes. These ideals are embodied in wabi-sabi-designed homes, which produce environments that are at once calm and intimately connected to nature. This section examines the qualities of wabi-sabi homes, emphasizing their materials, interior design, architectural features, and philosophical foundations that give them their distinctive style.

The architecture of wabi-sabi dwellings places a high value on harmony with the natural surroundings. These houses frequently use organic designs and natural materials that complement the surrounding environments in order to blend in well. The architecture prioritizes utility and simplicity over grandiosity and overbearing decoration. Wooden joinery is one of the many traditional Japanese building techniques used to create simple yet robust structures. Open spaces and a seamless transition between indoor and outdoor spaces are standard features of wabi-sabi home designs, which promote a feeling of oneness with nature.

Wabi-sabi interior design is characterized by a minimalist aesthetic that shies away from extravagance and clutter. The goal is to establish a serene, contemplative space that promotes mindfulness and introspection. There is not much furniture or décor—every item is picked for its beauty and usefulness. Things are frequently arranged asymmetrically to mimic the inherent randomness of the environment. In wabi-sabi design, the utilization of negative space, or ma, is essential because it creates a feeling of openness and breathing room in the house. A mood of serenity and reflection is produced by the deliberate balancing of space and simplicity.

Wabi-sabi homes emphasize the beauty of imperfection and the passage of time via the use of natural materials.

Because of their natural patinas and textures, organic materials like clay, stone, wood, and other materials are preferred. These materials are frequently displayed in their unadulterated beauty by being kept unprocessed or in their natural state. Common elements like dirt walls, rustic flooring, and wooden beams all add to the home's earthy, grounded atmosphere. Because the blemishes on these materials reveal something about the home's past and present, they are not concealed but rather appreciated. The essence of wabi-sabi aesthetics is a respect for age and imperfection that occurs naturally.

Typically, wabi-sabi homes have subdued color schemes that are inspired by the natural world. The predominant earth tones—browns, greens, grays, and soft whites—create a calming and well-balanced visual experience. The relationship between the house and its natural surroundings is strengthened by the use of these hues. Without overpowering the senses, depth and intrigue are added through the use of delicate color and texture variations. Because of the muted color scheme, the natural light and materials are able to shine through, adding to the peaceful atmosphere.

In wabi-sabi homes, light and shadow are carefully chosen because they are essential to achieving the right mood. Large windows, sliding doors, and open areas all help to optimize natural light, which lets the interior's atmosphere change with the light throughout the day. It is best to utilize soft, diffused light to highlight the textures and flaws in the materials and to create subtle contrasts. The play of light and shadow gives the area a dynamic character that is ever-changing and ever-evolving, much like the outside natural world.

Additionally, including characteristics of transience and impermanence, wabi-sabi homes serve as a reminder to their occupants of life's transient nature. Whether it's through floral arrangements, seasonal décor, or shifting window views, the house embraces and reflects the changing seasons. Because of their link to the natural cycles, residents are more mindful and present, which encourages them to enjoy the beauty of every moment. The acceptance of impermanence can also be seen in how the house is designed and maintained, where flaws and wear are acknowledged as essential components of the place's allure and character.

As extensions of the indoor living areas, gardens, and outdoor spaces are essential components of wabi-sabi homes. The same concepts of naturalness, imperfection, and simplicity inform the design of these gardens. Common elements that contribute to the timeless and harmonious mood of the landscape are aged wooden fences, stepping stones with uneven shapes, and stones covered in moss. The garden echoes the home's general aesthetic and philosophical elements by providing a space for introspection and a close relationship with nature.

The way of life and routines of the people who live in these houses are also influenced by the wabi-sabi concept. A slower, more intentional manner of life is encouraged by the emphasis on mindfulness and simplicity. Commonplace customs, like tea ceremonies or straightforward dinners, are handled with consideration and care, turning routine tasks into occasions for introspection and gratitude. A more profound sense of contentment and well-being is fostered by this attentive way of living since it increases people's awareness of the beauty of their surroundings and the present moment.

Handmade and artisanal items are everyday in wabi-sabi houses, which highlights the importance of originality and skill. Whether they be furniture, textiles, or pottery, these objects are selected for their individual characteristics and the tales they convey. These handcrafted items are appreciated for their faults, which lend a unique and human touch to the house. This respect for human touch and craftsmanship fits well with the larger wabi-sabi philosophy, which values imperfection and transience.

To sum up, wabi-sabi dwellings represent a deep and complex style that honors the beauty of simplicity, transience, and imperfection. These residences create environments that are peaceful, harmonious, and intimately connected to nature through their interior design, architecture, and use of natural materials. Wabi-sabi's philosophical foundations promote mindfulness, the present, and an appreciation of the beauty found in the transient and imperfect. By adhering to these ideas, wabi-sabi homes provide a haven from the hassles and diversions of contemporary living, encouraging a contented and peaceful lifestyle that is firmly anchored in the passing of time and the natural world.

Use of natural materials and asymmetry

In today's society, where people value sustainability, authenticity, and the beauty of imperfection more and more, the use of natural materials and asymmetry in design and construction has grown in importance. These ideas, which have their roots in many philosophical and cultural traditions, especially Japanese aesthetics like wabi-sabi, encourage a more thoughtful approach to living places and a closer relationship with the natural world. This section investigates the significance of asymmetry and natural materials in modern design, looking at their historical roots, practical and aesthetic advantages, and effects on how we interact with the built environment.

Since ancient times, natural materials have been employed in architecture and building due to their abundance, toughness, and inherent beauty. Reactions against the artificiality of contemporary commercial products and a desire for sustainable building methods have led to a resurgence of interest in these materials in recent years. Natural materials have several benefits, including clay, bamboo, stone, and wood. When compared to synthetic alternatives, they are renewable, biodegradable, and frequently need less energy to process. Furthermore, because they can control temperature and humidity and don't release any dangerous chemicals, they help create healthier interior settings.

Particularly wood is praised for both its practicality and visual attractiveness. Wood gives warmth and character to any area because each piece has a different grain pattern, color variety, and feel. Reclaimed wood has become more and more popular, supporting sustainable practices by conserving natural resources and cutting down on waste. Stone is another preferred material because of its unwavering strength and inherent beauty. Stone gives architectural and interior designs a sense of permanence and grounding, whether it is used in its raw state or polished as marble. Though less frequently utilized, clay and bamboo have distinctive textures and are essential to many cultures' ancient building methods.

Embracing irregularity and imperfection, asymmetry stands in stark contrast to the rigorous symmetry generally associated with classical Western design. This idea is fundamental to Japanese aesthetics, especially the concept of wabi-sabi, which finds beauty in the unfinished, ephemeral, and flawed. Asymmetry reflects the innate unpredictability of the natural world and gives an impression of dynamism and spontaneity. This method is used in traditional Japanese gardens, which steer clear of geometric perfection in favor of emulating natural landscapes with the placement of rocks, plants, and water features.

There are several ways that asymmetry can appear in both architecture and interior design. It is evident in the way spaces are laid out, with rooms and other components organized in a non-linear way to produce a more natural flow. Rather than using uniformity, furniture and decor pieces might be chosen for their distinctive shapes and irregularities, which can add to an overall sense of balance. Asymmetrical design departs from the rigidity and formality of symmetrical designs, promoting a more carefree and informal feel.

Using asymmetry and natural materials has many visual advantages. These guidelines make areas feel cozier, cozier, and more a part of the natural world. Because of their natural variances and flaws, natural materials provide interior spaces with a tactile feel that encourages contact and touch. Conversely, the use of asymmetry adds a feeling of surprise and fun, which makes areas more visually appealing and captivating. When combined, these components create a setting that is more dynamic and alive and captures the richness and beauty of the natural world.

Asymmetry and the use of natural materials have significant functional advantages that go beyond aesthetics. Natural materials frequently offer better performance qualities in areas like acoustics, durability, and thermal insulation. For instance, wood can contribute to energy efficiency by storing and releasing heat, which helps control indoor temperatures. Additionally, the thermal mass of stone may regulate indoor temperatures, keeping them warmer in the winter and colder in the summer. Because of its flexibility and ability to breathe, clay and bamboo can improve indoor air quality and offer comfort in a variety of conditions.

Through the encouragement of creative thinking and more effective use of available space, asymmetrical design can enhance functionality. Open-plan living rooms that effortlessly combine dining, cooking, and relaxing areas are examples of multifunctional spaces that can be created with non-linear layouts to suit a variety of demands. Because asymmetry frequently calls for custom solutions made for particular situations and purposes, it can also result in more ergonomic designs. This customized approach can improve a space's comfort and usability and increase its responsiveness to its occupants' requirements.

One should not undervalue the psychological effects of asymmetry and natural materials. Numerous studies have demonstrated the positive impact of being in nature on mood, stress reduction, and general well-being. The goal of biophilic design is to create places that link people with nature and improve both physical and mental health. It does this by incorporating natural materials and features into built environments. Natural materials' blemishes and imperfections can be soothing because they convey a sense of groundedness and authenticity. Asymmetry can inspire creativity and curiosity by breaking up the monotony of uniformity and enhancing the overall engaging and inspiring quality of a setting.

Asymmetry and the utilization of natural materials are also in line with more significant environmental and cultural ideals. These ideas are fundamental to building methods that emphasize environmental harmony and the preservation of natural resources in many traditional civilizations. Indigenous architecture frequently makes use of regionally produced materials and designs that adapt to the unique topography and climate of a location. This context-sensitive method encourages sustainable living and a sense of place by strengthening the bond between humans and their surroundings.

Asymmetry and the use of natural materials can be used in modern design as a counterpoint to the uniformity and homogenization that are frequently observed in settings that are mass-produced. It provides a chance to design environments that are distinctive, individual, and representative of personal interests and values. This method promotes a more careful and methodical approach to design and construction, emphasizing craftsmanship and quality over quantity and haste. Architects and designers may create physical environments that are not only aesthetically pleasing and practical but also meaningful and sustainable by giving priority to natural materials and asymmetrical design.

In conclusion, asymmetry and the use of natural materials in architecture and design are potent manifestations of authenticity, sustainability, and sophisticated aesthetics. These ideas, which have philosophical and cultural roots, honor the diversity of natural variances and the beauty of imperfection. Natural materials have several advantages, including their aesthetic and practical properties as well as their environmental sustainability. Asymmetry creates dynamic, spontaneous areas that are interesting and organic. When combined, these components create settings that are mellow, hospitable, and intimately tied to the natural world. Through the adoption of these ideas, modern design can encourage sustainability, well-being, and a more conscientious attitude to the built environment.

Incorporating Wabi-Sabi in contemporary art and design

Wabi-sabi, which emphasizes imperfection, impermanence, and incompleteness, is a Japanese aesthetic that can be used in modern art and design. Wabi-sabi, which has its roots in Zen Buddhism, is a philosophy that values simplicity, humility, and a profound respect for nature. This section examines the philosophical foundations of wabi-sabi, its influence on different art forms, and its applicability in contemporary culture, all while evaluating how contemporary artists and designers incorporate it into their work.

The idea of wabi-sabi contradicts Western notions of beauty, which frequently place a premium on consistency, symmetry, and perfection. Instead, it discovers beauty in the fleeting and the flawed. This philosophical perspective promotes a closer relationship to the organic cycles of life by being in harmony with the aging, degradation, and weathering processes that occur naturally. Wabi-sabi is a modern aesthetic that is exemplified by the use of organic materials, the appreciation of asymmetry, and a focus on handcrafted quality and authenticity.

Within the visual arts, wabi-sabi is evident in the creations of artists who value unprocessed, raw materials and impromptu, instinctive methods. This method stands in stark contrast to the refined, deliberate methods that are frequently preferred in conventional Western painting. For instance, the organic forms and noticeable hand marks of Japanese-American artist Isamu Noguchi's sculptures embody the concepts of wabi-sabi. The wabi-sabi philosophy of accepting imperfection and impermanence is embodied in Noguchi's use of natural materials like wood and stone.

In the same vein, wabi-sabi is frequently incorporated into the work of contemporary ceramic artists by highlighting the distinctive features of each piece. This idea is best shown by the Japanese craft of kintsugi, which entails fixing damaged ceramics using lacquer infused with powdered gold, silver, or platinum. By highlighting the beauty of their cracks, kintsugi turns shattered objects into something even more valuable than they would have been otherwise. Many contemporary ceramicists have been influenced by this technique, and they purposefully make works that include imperfections and cracks to highlight the beauty of imperfection.

Wabi-sabi concepts are used in interior design to create rooms that have a calm, grounded, and natural feel. This entails utilizing organic materials, such as clay, stone, and wood, which are frequently left in their unprocessed or barely processed forms. Simple and valuable furniture and décor pieces are selected, with a focus on handmade quality and workmanship. Typically, wabi-sabi interiors have a muted color scheme with earth tones and natural hues that come together to create a peaceful, harmonious space. Asymmetrical design avoids the stiff formality of symmetrical design and instead gives a feeling of spontaneity and vitality through layout and decor choices.

Japanese architect Tadao Ando's creations are a prominent illustration of wabi-sabi in modern design. Ando's designs frequently have noticeable flaws in the exposed concrete walls, giving them a raw, unfinished look that is in line with wabi-sabi aesthetics. Additionally, he uses natural light and shadows in his structures in ways that shift throughout the day to emphasize how fleeting the surroundings are. Ando's use of natural materials and straightforward shapes, along with his minimalist style, results in environments that inspire a deep sense of calm and reflection.

Wabi-sabi influences are evident in fashion through the use of organic materials, artisanal methods, and designs that celebrate imperfections. Fashion designers such as Comme des Garçons' Rei Kawakubo and Yohji Yamamoto frequently produce clothing that subverts conventional ideas of perfection and beauty. Their art has tattered edges, uneven cuts, and an overall look that embraces the temporary and the unfinished. In addition to adhering to wabi-sabi ideals, this method critiques the disposable, fast-paced character of contemporary fashion.

Wabi-sabi has influenced graphic design as well since the aesthetic values of naturalness, imperfection, and simplicity are used to produce visually striking pieces. To convey a feeling of uniqueness and authenticity, designers may employ organic shapes, textured backdrops, and hand-drawn elements. Another critical component of wabi-sabi in graphic design is the use of negative space, or ma, which lets the design breathe and directs the viewer's attention to the essential details. This understated style can stand out in a world that is frequently overtaken by highly detailed and sophisticated imagery.

Wabi-sabi encourages designers of products to focus on functionality and the beauty that comes from simplicity. Longevity and patina are prioritized in product design, enabling them to age beautifully and acquire personality over time. This stands in contrast to the current trend of intentional obsolescence and throwaway products. Because artisanal skill and handmade quality are highly valued, wabi-sabi-inspired objects frequently include a personal touch that adds significance for their owners.

The popularity of wabi-sabi in modern society can be attributed to people's desire for a more thoughtful lifestyle and their increasing understanding of environmental sustainability. Wabi-sabi, which emphasizes the importance of nature and the beauty of imperfection, provides a counterweight to a world where technology and mass manufacturing are becoming more and more dominant. It promotes a more leisurely, thoughtful way of living in which locations and things are valued for their individuality and relationship to the natural world.

Furthermore, wabi-sabi is in line with modern movements that support a simpler, more deliberate lifestyle, such as minimalism and slow living. Wabi-sabi encourages people to have a greater appreciation for their environment and the things they choose to surround themselves with by emphasizing what is genuinely beautiful and vital. A more sustainable way of life, where longevity and quality are prioritized over quantity and disposability, may result from adopting this concept.

To sum up, wabi-sabi requires a significant perspective change that values impermanence, imperfection, and simplicity in contemporary art and design. Wabi-sabi, which has its roots in Zen philosophy and Japanese aesthetics, promotes a closer relationship with nature as well as a more deliberate approach to the production and enjoyment of art and design. Wabi-sabi principles are employed in visual arts, ceramics, interior design, architecture, fashion, graphic design, and product design to encourage the use of natural materials, asymmetry, and a focus on trueness and skill. Wabi-sabi is a timeless and relevant approach that embraces the beauty of the flawed and the ephemeral at a time when society is becoming more and more concerned with mindfulness and sustainability. By using this lens, we can see how modern art and design can produce environments and items that are not only beautiful to look at but also profoundly meaningful and tied to the natural world.

Examples of Wabi-Sabi in modern architecture

A classic Japanese aesthetic idea, wabi-sabi celebrates the beauty of imperfection, impermanence, and the organic cycle of development and decay. This Zen-inspired worldview values authenticity and the passage of time while promoting respect for the unfinished and flawed. Although the origins of wabi-sabi are closely linked to traditional Japanese culture, its ideas have influenced many facets of modern design, specially building. This section examines the principles of wabi-sabi—simplicity, naturalness, and the acceptance of impermanence—as they relate to contemporary architecture using illustrative cases.

The Church of the Light in Ibaraki, Japan, designed by Tadao Ando, is among the most well-known instances of wabi-sabi in contemporary architecture. This 1989-completed building's natural materials and simplistic design perfectly capture the spirit of wabi-sabi. The church is a concrete building with a cross-shaped opening in the middle that lets light enter the interior. The way that light and shadow interact to produce this mood is peaceful and contemplative, which is in line with Wabi-sabi's emphasis on simplicity and the natural world. The unpolished, uneven concrete surfaces capture the essence of wabi-sabi, which values simplicity and unprocessed beauty. The building's architecture highlights the passing of time and the way light changes throughout the day, emphasizing the fundamental wabi-sabi idea of existence's transience.

The work of architect Kengo Kuma, whose designs frequently incorporate wabi-sabi aesthetics, is another noteworthy example. This method is demonstrated by Kuma's GC Prostho Museum Research Center, which was finished in 2010 in Kasugai, Japan. The building has a cypress wood lattice construction that not only blends in perfectly with the natural surroundings but also brings out the beauty of the faults in the wood. The choice of natural timber emphasizes the wabi-sabi idea of impermanence because it will age and change color over time. Kuma's design concept, which reflects the wabi-sabi ideal of fusing human works with the natural world, places a high priority on a harmonious link between the built environment and nature.

The method used by Belgian architect Vincent Van Duysen offers a modern take on the wabi-sabi concepts. The use of natural, frequently imperfect materials and simple, monolithic forms define Van Duysen's artistic style. For example, his Antwerp home is evidence of this aesthetic. Many ancient characteristics of the home, which was once a stable, have been preserved, including the exposed brick walls and wooden beams. These elements, which exhibit aging and wear, are embraced rather than hidden. The interior is functionally furnished in a minimalistic style, highlighting the wabi-sabi values of restraint and simplicity. A sense of peace and timeless elegance is created by the materials' patina and the subdued color scheme, encouraging residents to find beauty in the flawed and transient.

Architect Tom Kundig's designs in the US also appeal to wabi-sabi enthusiasts. Kundig, who is renowned for his rough, industrial style, frequently includes aspects that welcome change and imperfection. The Delta Shelter, a cabin in Washington State's woods, is one such instance. Built from weathering steel, the structure celebrates the wabi-sabi idea of natural decay by blending into the terrain as it gradually rusts and changes over time. With its big, movable shutters that enable direct interaction with the surroundings, the cabin's design is simple and practical. The raw, unfinished aspect of the materials and this dynamic connection with nature bring out the beauty of time and imperfection.

The Swiss architect Peter Zumthor, whose designs are renowned for their contemplative and sensory-rich styles, is another artist influenced by wabi-sabi. One famous example is the spa complex Therme Vals in Zumthor, Switzerland. Constructed on a mountainside using quartzite stone that is quarried nearby, the structure has a timeless and sturdy appearance. The stone's innate beauty is showcased by its natural variances and textures, which are left primarily untreated. The spa's design promotes a meditative experience that is in line with wabi-sabi concepts by encouraging guests to slow down and interact with their environment. A place that embraces the flawed and the fleeting is created by the focus on natural materials, the interplay of light and shadow, and the integration with the surroundings.

Apart from these architectural illustrations, adaptive reuse of buildings—the process of repurposing and revitalizing old structures—also exemplifies wabi-sabi ideals. This method preserves the original buildings' history and charm while also cutting down on trash. In the process of adaptive reuse, flaws that are prized for their authenticity and historical significance—such as cracks, patinas, and other aging indicators—are frequently preserved and emphasized. This approach is in line with the wabi-sabi appreciation of aging and the beauty inherent in decay and imperfection.

In summary, wabi-sabi has a significant and diverse impact on modern architecture, showing up in a variety of forms across a range of projects and methods. Around the world, architects are combining wabi-sabi ideas into their designs, as seen in the natural wood constructions of Kengo Kuma, the rustic, aged aesthetics of Tom Kundig, and the minimalist concrete forms of Tadao Ando. These illustrations show a shared love of natural materials, simplicity, and the beauty of imperfection, which promotes a closer relationship with the natural world and a contemplative understanding of life's fleeting nature. The ageless concept of wabi-sabi provides a valuable prism through which to design environments that are not just visually beautiful but also profoundly meaningful and compassionate as modern architecture develops.

CHAPTER III

Embracing Imperfection in Daily Life

Letting go of perfectionism

Perfectionism, which is sometimes praised as a virtue in cultures where competition is fierce, may also be a hefty weight that lowers one's quality of life and causes worry and burnout. Letting up perfectionism is about adopting a better, more balanced approach to both professional and personal development rather than renunciating high standards or a dedication to excellence. This section examines the negative impacts of perfectionism, its underlying roots, and doable tactics for developing a resilient and accepting mindset.

The relentless pursuit of flawlessness, frequently coupled with self-criticism and a fear of failing, is what defines perfectionism. Setting high expectations for yourself might inspire achievement, but perfectionism usually has unfavorable effects. The effect on mental health is among the most notable. Perfectionists are more likely to experience long-term stress, anxiety, and depression. Worry and unhappiness spiral out of control when there is continual pressure to live up to unrealistic expectations. Even minor errors or failures can lead to intense emotions of guilt and inadequacy, which feeds a destructive loop of perfectionistic thinking.

Perfectionism has many different roots, many of which can be traced back to early experiences and cultural influences. When parents give their children conditional approval—that is, praise based on accomplishments rather than inherent traits—they could teach their children that success determines their value. This idea has the potential to develop into perfectionistic behaviors over time. Pressures from society and culture can have a significant impact. Perfectionism can flourish in many societies where external accomplishments are frequently used to assess one's value and success. Social media makes matters worse by spreading unrealistic portrayals of happiness and success, which makes people feel inadequate and continually compare themselves to other people.

Realizing that perfection is an unachievable aim and becoming self-aware are the first steps toward letting go of perfectionism. This change in viewpoint enables people to reinterpret what success and self-worth are. To start this process, self-compassion practice is essential. Being self-compassionate entails being kind and understanding to oneself when you make errors or fall short. Acknowledging that imperfection is a common human experience, self-compassion fosters a supportive internal dialogue as an alternative to harsh self-criticism. This way of thinking builds resilience, which makes it possible for people to bounce back from setbacks and keep their well-being.

A different tactic for conquering perfectionism is to make flexible, attainable goals. Perfectionists frequently establish unreasonably high expectations that are unachievable, which causes dissatisfaction and disappointment. People might feel like they are making progress and have accomplished something by setting realistic goals and dividing more difficult jobs into smaller, more achievable steps. This strategy lessens the pressure to be faultless and promotes a more balanced pursuit of excellence by emphasizing effort and progress above flawless results.

Letting rid of perfectionism also requires embracing the idea of "good enough." This concept refutes the belief that only flawless results are worthwhile and emphasizes the value of completion and effort, even in the case of a subpar product. Having a "good enough" mindset can help people overcome the tension and anxiety that comes with perfectionism, allowing them to seek opportunities and take chances without worrying about failing. This mentality change encourages a more rewarding and long-lasting strategy for both career and personal development.

Meditation and mindfulness are effective strategies for overcoming perfectionism. Through the cultivation of present-moment awareness, these activities assist people in letting go of judgments and perfectionistic thoughts. People can get a better understanding of their perfectionistic inclinations and lessen their effects by objectively monitoring their thoughts and feelings. In contrast to the constant pursuit of perfection, mindfulness promotes acceptance of the current moment and cultivates a sense of serenity and contentment. Frequent mindfulness training can help remodel the brain, which will facilitate the adoption of a more compassionate and balanced way of living.

Getting help from others can also be a key component in conquering perfectionism. Talking about difficulties with close friends, family, or a therapist can help you gain critical perspective and support. People who are in supportive relationships feel understood and connected, which makes them know they are not alone in their experiences. For the purpose of treating the root reasons for perfectionism and creating more constructive coping strategies, therapy, in particular, might be helpful. Because it focuses on recognizing and correcting perfectionistic thought patterns and substituting them with more realistic and adaptable beliefs, cognitive-behavioral therapy (CBT) is particularly beneficial.

Learning to accept failure and mistakes as chances for improvement is another crucial component of letting go of perfectionism. Perfectionists frequently avoid strenuous activities or novel experiences because they believe that failure is a reflection of their own value. But failure is a necessary element of life and an essential aspect of growth and learning. Reframing failure as an opportunity for progress can help people develop a growth mindset, which prioritizes effort, tenacity, and ongoing improvement. This viewpoint promotes a more open-minded and daring outlook on life and lessens the fear of failing.

Gratitude exercises are another effective way to combat perfectionism. The emphasis is shifted from what is lacking or imperfect to what is already available and valued when one is grateful. Frequent reflection on life's good things—relationships, successes, and inner qualities, for example—promotes satisfaction and lessens the desire for perfection. Gratitude exercises, like writing in a gratitude diary or thanking people, can improve well-being and encourage a more contented and balanced viewpoint.

To sum up, getting rid of perfectionism necessitates a fundamental change in perspective and conduct. People can overcome the negative impacts of perfectionism and have more balanced, meaningful lives by embracing self-compassion, setting realistic objectives, assuming a "good enough" perspective, practicing mindfulness, getting assistance, accepting failure, and developing gratitude. It can be challenging to overcome deeply rooted perfectionistic tendencies, so patience and perseverance are needed on this road. But the benefits are well worth the work: stronger resilience, better mental health, and an increased sense of contentment and serenity. In the end, letting go of perfectionism enables people to accept and love their own selves—flaws and all—and to find happiness and fulfillment on the path rather than in the unachievable goal of perfection.

Creating Simple, Peaceful Spaces

The establishment of primary, tranquil areas in our homes and workplaces has become essential for improving well-being and cultivating mental clarity in an increasingly chaotic and fast-paced environment. These settings act as havens from the never-ending flood of information and stimuli, enabling people to find inner peace and reconnection with themselves. Creating such environments requires a deliberate use of natural materials, a simple design philosophy, and the incorporation of unique details that express the designer's taste and ideals. This section examines the fundamentals and advantages of designing uncomplicated, tranquil settings, providing information on how to accomplish them and the significant effects they can have on our lives.

The foundation of designing tranquil environments is simplicity. This idea, which is frequently connected to minimalist design, stresses getting rid of extraneous clutter and distractions. People can create a visually and mentally soothing environment by filling a place with only objects that have a purpose or make them happy. Being minimalistic is about making deliberate decisions about the things we surround ourselves with, not about leading a stark or austere life. Every object in a minimalist area should be essential and contribute to the overall harmony and functionality of the space. This method promotes mental clarity, lowers stress levels, and improves focus since it makes the surroundings mirror a more deliberate and orderly way of life.

An environment's ability to promote calm is greatly enhanced by the presence of natural elements. Natural fibers, stone, and wood can all help to establish a link to the outside world and foster a sense of calm and well-being. In this sense, using plants is incredibly beneficial. In addition to enhancing indoor air quality, plants bring a natural element that can have a calming and invigorating effect. Another vital element is natural light. Making the most of natural light by utilizing expansive windows, light-colored walls, and well-placed mirrors may help a room feel airier and more welcoming. Soft, warm artificial lighting can be used to create a calm and comfortable atmosphere in spaces with limited natural light.

A room's mood and ambiance are greatly influenced by its color scheme. Selecting soothing, neutral hues like whites, beiges, light grays, and pastels is advised for a serene atmosphere. These colors can give the impression of space and airiness while also having a calming impact. On the other hand, subtle color pops from artwork or accessories can offer character and warmth without overpowering the design's simplicity. The aim is to provide a harmonious, well-balanced appearance that encourages comfort and relaxation.

Picking out furniture is another important part of creating uncomplicated, tranquil settings. The simplicity of the space can be preserved by selecting furniture with simple shapes and lines. Fold-out desks and storage ottomans are two examples of multipurpose furniture that work well in compact spaces because they maximize space without adding clutter. Comfort and quality should take precedence over quantity when choosing furniture, making sure that each piece enhances the sensation of well-being as a whole. Cozy furnishings with soft textures, including linen drapes, woolen throws, and plush couches, can warm a room and provide comfort.

The secret to designing a room that is genuinely tranquil and cozy is personalization. As vital as simplicity and minimalism are, it's still critical to include things that are a reflection of individual preferences and recollections. This could consist of sentimental artwork, family photos, or trip mementos. These particular details elevate the room's emotional resonance and give it a distinctively yours. In order to keep the area uncluttered and full of meaning and significance, it is essential to find a balance between customization and simplicity.

The general tranquility of a space is also greatly influenced by its design and arrangement. An area that is neatly arranged, with everything in its proper position, can significantly lower stress and increase productivity. Innovative storage options like built-in cabinets, floating shelves, and storage baskets can help achieve this. Daily tasks can be made more doable and less daunting by keeping surfaces uncluttered and arranging objects logically. Moreover, optimizing the room's circulation and placing furnishings for user-friendliness can contribute to a more serene and well-organized atmosphere.

Creating uncomplicated, tranquil environments involves more than just the physical surroundings; it also involves adding sensory components that improve well-being and relaxation. For example, aromatherapy can have a significant effect on stress levels and mood. Aromas with relaxing qualities, such as eucalyptus, lavender, and chamomile, can be introduced by diffusers, candles, or essential oils. Another potent sensory component is sound. White noise, gentle background music, or natural sounds can all be used to create a calming aural environment that encourages calmness and relaxation.

There are numerous advantages to designing minimalist, serene environments. These settings can significantly enhance mental health by offering a haven from the strains of everyday life. They encourage awareness, which enables people to take deep breaths, settle down, and re-establish a connection with themselves. This can result in increased concentration, creativity, and output since calm, clutter-free environments encourage critical thinking and problem-solving. Additionally, tranquil areas can improve physical health by mitigating the harmful effects of stress, such as elevated blood pressure and compromised immune system. Better sleep is facilitated by a serene and well-organized setting, which is crucial for general health and well-being.

In conclusion, designing with mindfulness and an emphasis on natural materials, simplicity, and unique touches is the key to creating uncomplicated, tranquil environments. People can design spaces that support rest, mental clarity, and well-being by getting rid of clutter, selecting soothing colors and materials, and adding components that are a reflection of their beliefs. These areas have several advantages, including providing a haven from the craziness of the outer world and encouraging a sense of balance and inner serenity. Making austere, calm environments is becoming more than just a design decision as our lives get busier and more complicated; it's a necessary practice to improve our general health and quality of life.

Choosing meaningful, imperfect objects

Selecting meaningful, flawed items can be a potent act of resistance and a means of achieving greater personal fulfillment in a society where mass production and disposable consumer culture are becoming more and more prevalent. The Japanese aesthetic philosophy of wabi-sabi, which embraces imperfection, transience, and the beauty of the natural world, is the inspiration behind this method of choosing and cherishing possessions. By accepting the distinct imperfections and past of items, people can cultivate a more conscientious and intimate bond with their belongings. This section looks at the ideas behind selecting imperfect but meaningful objects, the advantages this practice has for the environment and psychology, and how it can be applied to daily life.

Wabi-sabi philosophy promotes an appreciation of the aging, the imperfect, and the real. This stands in stark contrast to the principles of newness, perfection, and disposability that are prevalent in today's commercial culture. Wabi-sabi encourages us to find beauty in patinas, cracks, and worn from usage and time. Selecting items that embody these attributes entails appreciating artistry, legacy, and the narratives encapsulated in the materials. With this viewpoint, our attention is diverted from outward appearances and toward our possessions' deeper, more profound relationships.

Developing attention is one of the main advantages of selecting imperfect yet meaningful objects. Being mindful entails appreciating the present moment and being totally present in it. We are encouraged to take our time and pay attention to the nuances when we choose and utilize defective objects. For example, a hand-thrown ceramic cup with an uneven glaze enables us to enjoy its tactile feel and recognize the distinct features that set it apart from similar factory-made items. This attentive interaction with our belongings can lower stress, boost happiness, and cultivate a more profound sense of gratitude.

In addition to having historical and personal value, meaningful but flawed items can improve our mental health. Antiques, handmade goods, and heirlooms frequently have backstories that link us to the people who created or once owned them. These items act as concrete connections to our history and sense of self. A grandmother's quilt, for instance, not only keeps you warm but also symbolizes affection and family history. These items become treasured representations of continuity and identity, providing solace and a feeling of home in the universe.

There are significant environmental benefits to selecting essential but imperfect goods. Waste, pollution, and resource depletion are only a few of the environmental problems brought on by mass production and the disposable society. The desire for new products and related ecological costs are decreased when we value and preserve old or flawed objects. The concepts of sustainability and responsible consumerism are in line with this approach. Reusing and mending items instead of throwing them away reduces waste even further and prolongs the life of materials. This strategy promotes a change to a more circular economy, where resources are used more carefully and intelligently.

A purposeful and careful approach to acquisition and utilization is necessary for bringing valuable, flawed goods into our lives. Take into account the new goods' provenance, craftsmanship, and narratives when choosing them. Choose vintage items that speak to your aesthetic and personal values or handmade gifts made by nearby artists. Make quality your top priority, and go for long-lasting, elegantly aging items. This leads to a more carefully chosen and significant collection of belongings, in addition to promoting sustainable techniques and talented craftspeople.

Looking through current possessions and recognizing those that have particular importance or distinctive flaws is one approach to getting started. Give these objects pride of position in your home and make frequent use of them. For example, a fractured vase that was gifted to you by a relative can serve as a focal point that evokes memories and discussions. You can strengthen the significance of these objects and improve your bond with them by actively interacting with and enjoying them.

Valuing defects also involves maintaining and repairing goods. Think about how something can be restored or repurposed instead of throwing it away because it is worn out or broken. Evident restorations, like the Japanese technique of kintsugi, which involves lacquering shattered ceramics with a mixture of gold, silver, or platinum, draw attention to the object's past and enhance its beauty. This activity not only prolongs the life of material belongings but also cultivates a resilient and creative mindset. It promotes finding worth and potential in things that might otherwise be viewed as defective or pointless.

A home's vibe can be changed by furnishing it with meaningful but flawed objects. It creates a feeling of warmth and genuineness that is frequently absent from rooms full of impersonal, mass-produced objects. Every item has a backstory and adds to a distinct, individual tale. This might strengthen the feeling that one's house is a haven, a place where one can fully unwind and feel connected to what's essential.

Additionally, this strategy may impact more general attitudes and lifestyle decisions. A more accepting and sympathetic perspective of oneself and other people can result from embracing flaws and placing a higher value on significance than perfection. It opposes the demands of society to live up to unattainable ideals of perfection and promotes a more sincere and compassionate way of life. This change can foster a better self-image, strengthen bonds with others, and lessen feelings of inadequacy.

Selecting imperfect but significant items also encourages a slower, more deliberate pace of life. It promotes taking a vacation from the never-ending rush of contemporary life and the never-ending quest for newer, faster, better things. By appreciating what we already have and looking for objects with character and significance, we make room for introspection, thankfulness, and a greater understanding of the here and now. We may make more deliberate decisions and feel more in control of our buying patterns because of this slower pace.

In summary, selecting imperfect but meaningful objects is a behavior that has significant positive effects on the environment, psychology, and way of life. This method, which has its roots in the wabi-sabi philosophy, places a premium on genuineness, artistry, and the backstories that come with our belongings. It encourages a more deliberate and unified way of living by fostering mindfulness, mental health, and sustainability. We can design environments and lifestyles that are more meaningful, richer, and consistent with our actual values by accepting faults and emphasizing the underlying meaning of the possessions we own. This change improves our own well-being and makes the world a more caring and sustainable place.

Rituals and routines that foster a Wabi-Sabi mindset

The Wabi-Sabi ideology honors the beauty of impermanence, imperfection, and the organic cycle of growth and decay. It has its roots in Zen Buddhism and Japanese aesthetics. A deep respect for modesty, simplicity, and the subtle elegance present in daily life is fostered by this perspective. In order to help people adopt a more conscious, balanced, and genuine way of life, it is essential to develop rituals and routines that are in line with the Wabi-Sabi philosophy. In order to foster a Wabi-Sabi mindset and increase one's appreciation for the imperfect and fleeting quality of existence, this section examines a variety of rituals and routines.

Being wholly present and involved in the present moment is a practice known as mindfulness, and it is one of the core components of a Wabi-Sabi attitude. Daily meditation is a powerful technique for bringing oneself back to the present and cultivating mindfulness. By encouraging acceptance and non-judgment, meditation fosters an awareness of ideas, feelings, and sensations. People can develop a closer relationship with both their inner selves and the outside environment by setting aside some time each day to sit still and pay attention to their breath. Two of the central tenets of the Wabi-Sabi philosophy are satisfaction and peace, which are fostered by this practice.

Including mindful eating in everyday activities can help cultivate a Wabi-Sabi attitude. This entails enjoying every bite, being cognizant of the act of eating, and recognizing the flavors, textures, and fragrances of food. Those who eat mindfully and slowly can develop an appreciation for the sustenance that their food provides. In addition to improving the sensory aspects of eating, this practice fosters a closer relationship with the producers of food and the labor-intensive process of preparing it. Eating with awareness turns a routine task into a meaningful ritual that respects life's simplicity and impermanence.

Another Wabi-Sabi heritage activity that is firmly ingrained is participating in tea rituals. The highly ritualized Japanese tea ceremony, known as "chanoyu," represents the values of peace, harmony, decency, and quiet. Matcha is powdered green tea, and participants prepare and drink it with an emphasis on mindfulness and appreciating the present moment. A profound sense of calm and connection is fostered by the meticulous attention to every detail, from whisking the tea to cleaning the dishes. People can embrace the Wabi-Sabi worldview by incorporating aspects of this ritual into their daily lives, such as making time to drink tea mindfully and intentionally.

Another good technique to develop a Wabi-Sabi mindset is to declutter and create a minimalist living area. This is getting rid of everything that isn't needed and emphasizing practicality and simplicity. People can make their surroundings more calm and harmonious—which embodies the Wabi-Sabi ideals of imperfection and simplicity—by cleaning. A living area can be made into a haven of peace and clarity by limiting the number of things in it to only those that you enjoy or that are useful. This procedure promotes a move away from materialism and in the direction of a deeper understanding of the inherent worth of every item.

One can also cultivate a Wabi-Sabi mindset by partaking in creative endeavors that prioritize process over perfection. Art forms like calligraphy, gardening, and ceramics all incorporate elements of imperfection and unpredictability by nature. For instance, when creating pottery, the artist's handprints and the inherent variances in the materials are frequently visible, creating one-of-a-kind works. Regardless of the result, accepting these flaws as a necessary part of the creative process can help people see the intrinsic worth of their work and the beauty of the process itself. Resilience and a greater understanding of life's organic cycle are fostered by this way of thinking.

One of the most effective ways to integrate Wabi-Sabi is to establish a connection with nature. Impermanence and imperfection in its purest form are embodied in nature. Spending time in outdoor environments on a regular basis can improve one's appreciation of the fleeting beauty of the natural world, whether by trekking, strolling, or just relaxing in a garden. Harmony and acceptance are fostered by observing the passing of time, the growth and decay of plants, and the minute changes in the surroundings. These encounters serve as a reminder to people of their place in the larger cycles of life as well as the beauty found in imperfection and change.

A Wabi-Sabi mindset can be further enhanced by daily thankfulness rituals. You can develop a greater sense of appreciation and contentment by setting aside some time each day to think about and be grateful for the little things in life that are sometimes taken for granted. Keeping a thankfulness diary, where people list a few things for which they are thankful every day, is one way to engage in this practice. People might adopt a mindset that accepts and revels in the flawed and fleeting nature of existence by concentrating on the pleasant aspects of life, no matter how minor.

Developing a Wabi-Sabi mindset also requires engaging in self-compassion practices. Treating oneself with the same consideration and understanding that one would extend to a friend is a critical component of self-compassion. People are encouraged by this approach to accept their own flaws and vulnerabilities without passing judgment on them. People can cultivate a better relationship with themselves and lessen the pressure to live up to unattainable expectations of perfection by adopting self-compassion. The Wabi-Sabi philosophy, which emphasizes authenticity and the beauty of imperfection, is in line with this way of thinking.

Including slow living techniques in everyday tasks can also help cultivate a Wabi-Sabi attitude. A more thoughtful and intentional way of living is emphasized by slow living, which values meaningful experiences over material belongings and places an emphasis on quality over quantity. This can entail making schedule adjustments, cutting back on obligations, and making more time for relaxation, introspection, and spending time with close friends and family. People can design a more contented and balanced existence that adheres to the Wabi-Sabi ideals by slowing down and concentrating on what really matters.

In summary, incorporating rituals and practices that value impermanence, mindfulness, and simplicity is essential to cultivating a Wabi-Sabi worldview. A more profound sense of contentment and harmony can be attained by practices including meditation, mindful eating, tea ceremonies, decluttering, artistic endeavors, spending time in nature, being grateful, practicing self-compassion, and living slowly. People can develop a mindset that appreciates the beauty of the present moment and the intrinsic value of the flawed and fleeting aspects of existence by implementing these routines into their daily lives. This change in viewpoint promotes a more genuine and meaningful way of life in addition to improving personal well-being.

Integrating Wabi-Sabi principles into everyday activities

The Japanese aesthetic theory of Wabi-Sabi, which has its roots in Zen Buddhism, honors the natural cycles of development and decay as well as the beauty of imperfection and impermanence. Awakening to the fleeting and flawed aspect of life, practicing mindfulness, and embracing simplicity are all part of incorporating Wabi-Sabi ideals into daily activities. This section investigates how incorporating these ideas into everyday activities can promote a more aware, fulfilled, and peaceful way of life.

Cultivating mindfulness is a key component of incorporating Wabi-Sabi into daily life. Being mindful is living in the present moment with all of your senses, which can make even the most routine tasks meaningful. Take the easy task of cleaning dishes, for instance. By being attentive of the warm water's sensations, the soap's texture, and the act of cleaning each dish, one can approach the task without hurrying through it. This attentive method cultivates a sense of serenity and presence that extends throughout the rest of the day, in addition to making the activity more enjoyable.

Wabi-Sabi principles can also change how food is prepared and enjoyed. Slowing down, enjoying every bite, and recognizing the flavors, textures, and fragrances of the meal are all encouraged by mindful eating. Mealtime turns into a mindful activity that brings us into the present by emphasizing the sensory aspects of eating and feeling thankful for the sustenance it offers. Additionally, cooking straightforward, healthful meals and selecting seasonal, locally produced products are in line with the Wabi-Sabi love of nature and its cycles.

Another approach to incorporate Wabi-Sabi into daily life is to include it into one's home surroundings. Decluttering and designing an area that prioritizes utility and simplicity will help achieve this. One can choose to fill a home with handcrafted, artisanal products that showcase individual artistry and distinctive faults, as opposed to accumulating mass-produced items. For example, the Wabi-Sabi values of authenticity and imperfection are embodied in a piece of reclaimed wood furniture or a hand-thrown ceramic bowl. These things give a house a feeling of coziness and character, transforming it into a simple haven of peace.

A useful pastime that perfectly embodies Wabi-Sabi concepts is gardening. Taking care of plants and witnessing their development, deterioration, and regrowth helps us understand the life's natural cycles. A garden can be made to celebrate the beauty of imperfection and impermanence by letting it grow naturally with native plants and wildflowers. It doesn't have to be precisely maintained. Gardening promotes attention and offers a concrete means of experiencing the seasonal changes, which deepens one's understanding of nature's cycles.

Wabi-Sabi can also improve daily routines such as self-care and personal grooming. These routines can be viewed as chances for mindfulness and self-compassion, rather than as duties. For example, dedicating some time to a basic skincare regimen might turn into a calming practice that helps us feel centered and grounded. Using organic, less processed goods might also be in line with the Wabi-Sabi aesthetic, which values simplicity and authenticity. Those who approach self-care as an opportunity to nurture themselves rather than as a chore to be finished might develop a more profound feeling of contentment and well-being.

One of the best ways to incorporate Wabi-Sabi ideas into daily life is through creative endeavors. Art forms including calligraphy, knitting, painting, and ceramics inherently incorporate elements of imperfection and unpredictability. A more rewarding and genuine creative experience might result from accepting these flaws as a necessary component of the creative process. In ceramics, for instance, the distinctive blemishes and flaws of hand-thrown objects are cherished as essential components of their charm and individuality. This way of thinking promotes appreciating each creation's individuality and authenticity rather than striving for perfection.

Wabi-Sabi can enhance the basic yet deep activity of walking. Walking every day gives you the chance to slow down and pay attention to your surroundings, whether you're in the city or the countryside. A profound appreciation for the beauty of the present moment can be fostered by observing the shifting seasons, the play of light and shadow, and the minute nuances that are frequently overlooked. Strolling aimlessly for the sheer joy of movement and observation can develop into a contemplative activity that fosters a Wabi-Sabi mentality.

Daily interactions can be improved by incorporating Wabi-Sabi ideas into relationships and communication. In talks, placing a strong emphasis on acceptance, vulnerability, and authenticity encourages deeper understanding and connections. This method promotes appreciating each person's individuality and accepting them for who they are in relationships. People can develop deeper and more satisfying relationships by listening empathetically, expressing themselves honestly, and being present and attentive throughout talks.

Wabi-Sabi concepts can also be beneficial in one's professional and work life. Stress can be decreased, and satisfaction can be raised by approaching jobs mindfully and with an emphasis on the process rather than perfection. Accepting that errors and setbacks are a necessary component of learning and development in the workplace entails embracing imperfection. People with this perspective are more resilient and creative, which makes it easier for them to adapt and develop. Increasing productivity and well-being can be achieved by establishing a work environment that prioritizes clarity, simplicity, and purpose.

Last but not least, incorporating Wabi-Sabi into regular tasks calls for a mental adjustment toward appreciation and acceptance. This entails seeing the beauty in the flawed and fleeting facets of life and learning to appreciate them. A greater feeling of contentment and serenity can be fostered by cultivating appreciation by recognizing the little, frequently disregarded benefits of everyday existence. For instance, one might develop a more resilient and upbeat mindset by setting aside some time each day to consider and express gratitude for all of the good things in life, no matter how minor.

To sum up, applying the concepts of Wabi-Sabi to daily life entails accepting attention, simplicity, and an understanding of impermanence and imperfection. These ideas can make routine activities meaningful rituals, whether through mindful eating, decluttering, gardening, personal hygiene, artistic endeavors, walking, communication, career life, or practicing thankfulness. A Wabi-Sabi worldview allows people to discover fulfillment and beauty in life's imperfections and transience, leading to a more aware, content, and harmonious way of living. This change of viewpoint not only improves one's own well-being but also fosters a more genuine and social lifestyle.

CHAPTER IV

Nurturing Relationships through Wabi-Sabi

Accepting Imperfection in Others

The foundation of interpersonal relationships and personal development is the ability to accept others' imperfections. This idea entails accepting each person for who they are, with all of their quirks and imperfections. It is an essential ability that promotes compassion, empathy, and closer relationships between individuals. We can create a society that is more accepting, tolerant, and peaceful if we accept that imperfection is a natural part of being human.

Realizing that no one is flawless is the first step towards embracing imperfections. Acknowledging this fact is frequently easier said than done because personal expectations and cultural influences can impair our judgment. A lot of people are raised with expectations of perfection from their families, the media, and society at large. Unrealistic expectations for achievement, behavior, and attractiveness are produced by these ideals. Feelings of disappointment, irritation, and even animosity can result when others fail to live up to these expectations. But when we acknowledge that everyone is flawed, we make room for a more sincere and caring comprehension of those around us.

An essential component of this process is empathy. Empathy is experiencing another person's emotions, ideas, and viewpoints by placing oneself in their position. We can have a deeper understanding of the motivations behind someone's actions and behaviors by practicing empathy. Many times, the things that we consider to be defects or shortcomings are actually just variations in experiences, backgrounds, and life challenges. Empathy enables us to see past appearances and recognize the depth of the human experience.

Self-reflection is a crucial component of embracing imperfection. Before we can truly accept the flaws and limits of others, we must first acknowledge our own. It can be challenging to reach this degree of humility and self-awareness. Recognizing our own shortcomings helps us to be more understanding and forgiving of others. Healthy relationships are built on this self-acceptance because we are less prone to transfer our fears and irrational expectations onto other people.

Fostering acceptance also requires effective communication. People can voice their opinions and concerns in a courteous, open, and honest conversation without worrying about being judged. People are more willing to open up and disclose who they really are when they feel heard and understood. Since it fosters a secure environment for vulnerability, this authenticity deepens relationships and increases trust. Furthermore, good communication lessens the negative effects of perceived flaws by resolving confrontations and clearing up misunderstandings.

Accepting others' imperfections has wider social ramifications in addition to improving interpersonal connections. Social harmony and cohesion in varied and multicultural cultures depend on acceptance of diversity. Biases and prejudices can result from a failure to recognize and accept the flaws in other people. We may fight prejudice and advance inclusivity by valuing variety and realizing that each person has particular talents and shortcomings. In consequence, this promotes a more just and equal society in which people are respected for their intrinsic worth as opposed to being assessed according to subjective norms.

Moreover, the idea of unconditional love is strongly related to the acceptance of imperfection. Loving someone unconditionally is accepting them for who they are, faults and all. This kind of love is necessary for both romantic and familial relationships because it offers a solid basis for long-lasting bonds. Unconditional love entails a dedication to encouraging and assisting each other in growing despite flaws rather than disregarding or justifying negative behavior. It is a love that honors each person's individuality and perseveres in the face of adversity.

Accepting imperfections has positive effects on one's mental and emotional health. Excessive criticism of others can cause tension in our relationships and cause stress and unhappiness. On the other hand, accepting imperfections frees people from the need to live up to unattainable ideals, resulting in more sincere and satisfying relationships. By teaching us to value others for who they really are rather than for what we wish them to be, it fosters a sense of serenity and satisfaction.

In the workplace, efficiency and teamwork can be improved by accepting imperfection. Acknowledging the distinct abilities and viewpoints of each team member can result in more creative ideas and a more encouraging work atmosphere. Leaders who appreciate and embrace their subordinates' flaws are more likely to engender drive and loyalty. They foster an environment of transparency and ongoing development where errors are viewed as chances for development and learning rather than as failures.

Tolerating damaging or abusive behavior does not equate to accepting imperfection, though. It's critical to discern between flaws that don't pose a severe risk to oneself or others and those that do. Respect and safety in partnerships are contingent upon the establishment of sound boundaries. Acceptance shouldn't be sacrificed for someone's honesty or general well-being.

In conclusion, learning to accept others' imperfections is a complex process that calls for communication, self-reflection, empathy, and unconditional love. It's a technique that improves interpersonal connections, fosters harmony in society, and supports mental and emotional health. We can create a more compassionate and inclusive environment and forge more robust, more genuine connections by accepting and valuing the flaws that make us human. Although the path to acceptance is not always straightforward, it is worthwhile since it enriches and deepens our lives.

Building deeper, more authentic connections

Developing more meaningful and genuine relationships is essential to people's happiness and contentment. Building authentic relationships takes conscious work and self-awareness at a time when digital interactions frequently trump in-person contacts. Genuine relationships entail a deep comprehension and acceptance of oneself as well as others and transcend surface-level interactions. People can form deep connections that improve their own lives as well as the lives of people around them by encouraging openness, empathy, and active participation.

Self-awareness is the first step towards developing more profound connections. Comprehending one's beliefs, aspirations, and anxieties is essential for genuine communication. People can show their true selves to others when they are in tune with their inner selves. Because of their genuineness, they draw in like-minded others who respect and identify with their actual selves. Recognizing and overcoming one's own obstacles to connection, such as fears or traumatic experiences, is another aspect of self-awareness. Relationships that are more genuine and meaningful are facilitated by this process of reflection and personal development.

Being vulnerable is essential to creating genuine connections. It entails sharing one's thoughts, feelings, and experiences with others—even when doing so seems risky or uncomfortable. Being vulnerable communicates a desire to be seen and appreciated for who they really are, which in turn promotes intimacy and trust. By being open to people, you foster a reciprocal exchange of authenticity. Vulnerability must be wisely used, though, as disclosing too much too soon might overwhelm or alienate others. A balance between openness and respect for one's personal space is necessary to forge stronger friendships.

Real connections require empathy, or the capacity to comprehend and experience another person's emotions. Active listening and a sincere interest in the feelings and experiences of another person are prerequisites for empathy. To genuinely comprehend another person's viewpoint, one must set aside their own preconceptions and judgments. People can foster a secure and encouraging environment where others feel appreciated and understood by engaging in empathy practices. Mutual comprehension strengthens ties between individuals and promotes a feeling of connection and belonging.

Another essential component of creating stronger ties is active participation. This entails giving conversations your whole attention, participating fully, and demonstrating a sincere interest in the other person. Distractions like social media and cell phones make it simple to lose focus and get disengaged in today's environment. However, deliberate and concentrated interaction is necessary for genuine connections. Reducing outside distractions, keeping eye contact, and contributing to the discourse are ways to accomplish this. Engaging in active communication shows gratitude and respect, which strengthens the relationship's sincerity.

Deeper connections can also be strengthened through shared activities and experiences. Traveling, volunteering, or taking up a shared activity are examples of meaningful activities that can foster relationships and produce cherished memories. These interactions create a sense of unity and lay the groundwork for more in-depth discussions and relationships. Furthermore, overcoming obstacles and striving for shared objectives can deepen relationships by fostering a sense of cooperation and support among participants.

Sincere relationships are fundamentally based on honesty. Even in the face of difficulty, being honest with others fosters honesty and trust in the partnership. Being honest requires discussing one's thoughts, feelings, and boundaries in a courteous and straightforward manner. It also entails being truthful with oneself regarding one's requirements and preferences in a partnership. A relationship can thrive when there is a shared commitment to honesty between the two sides.

Forging deeper ties also requires acceptance and forgiveness. Believing that everyone is fallible and imperfect is necessary to keep interactions honest. Connections might be hampered by unreal expectations or clinging to grudges. As an alternative, cultivating acceptance and forgiveness promotes a kind and understanding atmosphere. This entails accepting human frailty and being prepared to resolve disputes and misunderstandings with grace and empathy rather than condoning bad behavior.

Furthermore, real connections require the maintenance of boundaries. Boundaries safeguard an individual's welfare and guarantee courteous and reciprocal exchanges. They entail expressing one's boundaries in a straightforward manner and honoring those of others. Intimacy and individualism can coexist in harmony when there are healthy boundaries, fostering stronger ties without compromising moral principles. Respecting limits helps to build trust and a sense of security in a partnership.

Time and patience are also necessary for creating stronger connections. Genuine connections take time to establish; they must be worked on and maintained consistently. Over time, a relationship is strengthened when both parties take the time to get to know one another, share stories, and offer support during difficult times. Deeper friendships frequently necessitate resolving misconceptions, disputes, and obstacles. Therefore, patience is crucial. People can develop relationships that are meaningful and long-lasting by making a commitment to one another and pushing through challenges.

Developing stronger ties has wider societal ramifications in addition to personal ones. Genuine relationships help communities and organizations feel like they belong and have a common goal. They foster an environment that is encouraging and welcoming, making people think meaningful and inspired. Consequently, this improves teamwork, innovation, and general well-being. People make a more caring and cohesive community by encouraging more significant relationships in all areas of life.

In summary, developing more genuine and profound connections is a complex process that calls for self-awareness, openness, empathy, active participation, forgiveness, acceptance, boundaries, time, and patience. These components lay the groundwork for sincere and meaningful connections that improve people's lives and promote a sense of fulfillment and belonging. A significant and fulfilling pursuit, pursuing authenticity and deeper relationships, is essential in a world where surface-level interactions are the norm. We can make the world a more compassionate and connected place where everyone is respected and feels seen for who they really are by practicing these traits within ourselves and in our relationships.

The value of silence and non-verbal communication

We frequently undervalue the importance of quiet and nonverbal communication in our fast-paced, technologically connected world, where words and technology rule relationships. Nonetheless, nonverbal clues and silence are practical components of human communication that can express intentions, feelings, and thoughts in ways that words alone are unable to. These communication-related facets are essential for developing empathy, comprehending and connecting with others, and strengthening the depth of our bonds with one another.

In all of its manifestations, silence is a powerful means of conveying feelings and ideas. It can be a potent tool for introspection, letting people analyze their ideas and emotions without feeling compelled to answer right away or communicate orally. Silence during a conversation can foster introspection and a deeper understanding by allowing both participants to take in and consider what has been said. This is not a silent place; instead, it is a place full of possibilities and significance. It can convey a variety of feelings, including respect, anticipation, and melancholy. For instance, a period of silence during a memorial service honors the deceased and offers an incognito place for mourning and remembering without requiring words.

More information is frequently communicated nonverbally than verbally. Nonverbal cues include posture, eye contact, facial expressions, and body language. Studies indicate that a substantial amount of human communication occurs through nonverbal means. For example, facial expressions transcend language borders and are generally recognized to indicate emotions like happiness, sadness, rage, or surprise. A grin, a furrowed brow, an eyebrow raised, or a tear can instantly convey a wide range of complicated feelings and sentiments. These nonverbal clues are essential for building rapport and trust because they offer instantaneous responses and bolster spoken messages. In a conversation, for example, a pleasant grin can increase the sense of comfort and connection, whereas crossed arms can convey defensiveness or disagreement even when the words are neutral.

Another important aspect of nonverbal communication is body language. It consists of posture, motions, and gestures that support, accentuate, or contradict spoken words. For instance, leaning forward during a discussion usually denotes engagement and attention, whereas leaning back could imply disengagement or indifference.

Nodding, pointing, and other hand gestures are examples of gestures that can emphasize and make spoken words more understandable. When reading, body language, context, and cultural background are equally important factors to consider. In certain cultures, a gesture that is deemed kind could be seen as offensive. Therefore, for cross-cultural relationships to be productive, it is imperative to comprehend the subtleties of non-verbal communication.

Making eye contact is a subtle yet effective way to communicate nonverbally. It communicates curiosity, attention, and sincerity. While avoiding eye contact could be interpreted as uncomfortable, dishonesty, or apathy, maintaining acceptable eye contact during a conversation demonstrates that you are involved and attentive. Cultural standards about eye contact, however, differ significantly. Direct eye contact can be interpreted as impolite or aggressive, depending on the culture. In others, it is a sign of sincerity and confidence. In today's globalized world, understanding these cultural distinctions is essential for efficient communication.

Negotiation and conflict resolution also heavily rely on silence and nonverbal cues. Silence may be a very effective de-escalation technique in heated circumstances because it gives people time to gather their thoughts and cool down before acting. It gives everyone a chance to collect themselves, which lessens the possibility of hurried or hostile reactions. Nonverbal cues like keeping your shoulders back, speaking in a soft voice and nodding to indicate understanding can all assist in easing tension and establish rapport, which in turn can lead to more fruitful conversations. Silence and body language can be utilized strategically in negotiations to communicate openness, patience, and confidence, which frequently results in better outcomes.

Additionally, the benefits of silence and nonverbal communication can be seen in therapeutic contexts, where it can play a crucial role in self-discovery and healing. Silence is a standard tool in psychotherapy to help clients think about their feelings and thoughts without being interrupted by spoken cues. This place of reflection can result in profound realizations and emotional breakthroughs. Nonverbal clues from therapists, such as keeping an open posture, nodding, and maintaining eye contact, communicate empathy and understanding, and foster a secure space where clients feel free to express themselves.

The value of quiet and nonverbal communication has increased in the digital age, when social media contacts, emails, and texts predominate. The intricacies of in-person communication are frequently absent from digital communication, which can result in misconceptions and misinterpretations. While video calls, gifs, and emojis are some of the technologies used to close this gap, they are still unable to fully capture the depth of non-verbal cues that are present in face-to-face communication. Therefore, in order to maintain clear and compassionate communication, it is crucial to be aware of the silence and other non-verbal cues in digital encounters.

In conclusion, it is impossible to overestimate the importance of silence and nonverbal cues. These components are essential to human interaction because they increase the breadth, genuineness, and potency of our relationships. While non-verbal cues enhance communication by expressing feelings, intentions, and attitudes beyond words, silence offers a space for introspection and emotional processing. We may create deeper connections that go beyond the confines of spoken language, resolve disagreements more skillfully, and forge stronger, more sympathetic relationships by understanding and utilizing the power of silence and nonverbal communication. By doing this, we improve our capacity for empathy and understanding, which enriches our interactions and strengthens our bonds with others.

Fostering honest and simple interactions

Establishing frank and straightforward exchanges is crucial for developing real connections, encouraging efficient communication, and creating an environment of mutual respect and trust. Setting the importance of honest and direct communication above complexity and superficiality can result in more meaningful interactions, improved teamwork, and a more satisfying human experience in a society that frequently lacks these things. To do this, we must make a commitment to openness, compassion, and attentive listening—all of which enhance the genuineness of our exchanges.

The foundation of every meaningful interaction is honesty. It entails speaking the truth, even when it is challenging or uncomfortable, about our goals, feelings, and ideas. Honest communication builds the trust that serves as the cornerstone of wholesome relationships. Knowing that they are engaging with someone who values and appreciates their knowledge and worth gives people a sense of security and worth. Since it removes the need for conjecture and assumptions, honest communication helps to avoid misunderstandings and misinterpretations. We provide others with the knowledge they need to respond effectively and meaningfully when we communicate our thoughts and feelings in a clear and concise manner.

Conversely, straightforward conversations necessitate succinctness and clarity in communication. Maintaining simplicity in our communication guarantees that our messages are clear and prevent misunderstandings. This does not imply that we should have less sophisticated discourse; instead, we should concentrate on having concise, direct communication that goes right to the point. Simple interactions cut down on the noise and distraction that come from verbose or extremely complex communication. They make communication more accessible and more productive, preventing the central point from being obscured by extraneous information or technical terms.

When we combine simplicity with honesty, our interactions become much better. We respect the other person's time and intelligence when we speak in an open and straightforward manner. We recognize that they are capable of appreciating honesty and the truth. This strategy promotes open communication and respect for one another, which leads to a more cooperative and encouraging atmosphere. When people believe that their interactions are founded on honesty and transparency, they are more inclined to participate and make a significant contribution.

In order to promote straightforward and honest communication, empathy is essential. Understanding and sharing the emotions of others is a necessary component of empathy, which fosters the development of relationships based on respect and understanding. Since we realize the importance of truth in promoting understanding and trust, we are more inclined to communicate honestly when we approach conversations with empathy. Simplicity is also encouraged by empathy, as we try to communicate in a way that is thoughtful and understandable to the other person. We can adjust our communication to be open and honest by placing ourselves in the other person's shoes.

Another essential element of encouraging straightforward and honest communication is active listening. Engaging fully with the speaker, observing their words, tone, and body language, and intelligently replying are all components of active listening. This reinforces the importance of being honest in communication by showing respect and appreciation for the viewpoints of others. We are better able to comprehend the main points of the message and reply in a direct and honest way when we attentively listen. The quality of the contact is further improved by actively listening, which also helps to resolve any ambiguities and guarantees that both parties are on the same page.

Setting up a setting that promotes straightforward communication and honesty needs deliberate work and dedication to particular values. Among these is the idea of transparency. Being honest about our aims, motivations, and any pertinent information is a sign of being transparent in our communication. Openness promotes trust and lessens the possibility of miscommunication. It sends a message to others that we respect their right to know the truth and that we have nothing to conceal.

Respect is an additional tenet. Treating people with dignity and appreciating their viewpoints and experiences are essential components of respect. Being honest and direct is more common when we speak with respect because we understand how important these traits are to preserving a civil relationship. Respect also entails being cognizant of and grateful for the time and effort invested in the other person, which promotes ease in our interactions.

Another essential component of encouraging straightforward and sincere conversations is vulnerability. To be vulnerable is to be open to expressing our actual feelings and thoughts, even when doing so leaves us feeling exposed or uneasy. Authenticity and trust are fostered by vulnerability since it demonstrates our willingness to be forthright and honest. By being open and honest with one another, we make room for more sincere and meaningful relationships.

Establishing straightforward and sincere communication is beneficial in many spheres of life, such as intimate partnerships, workplaces, and public spaces. These exchanges establish a foundation of knowledge and trust in interpersonal relationships, which strengthens bonds and increases emotional closeness. Since it promotes open communication and respect for one another, straightforward and honest communication helps to resolve issues more successfully. Additionally, it lessens the tension and worries that are frequently brought on by miscommunications and covert objectives.

In business settings, encouraging straightforward and sincere communication can improve productivity and teamwork. Team members are better equipped to work together and support one another when they speak honestly and clearly. People feel appreciated and respected in an environment of accountability and openness that is fostered by honest communication. Since employees are more willing to invest in an atmosphere that values honesty and clarity, this raises engagement and motivation levels.

Honest and straightforward relationships foster a more supportive and cohesive group. Because they make people feel like they are part of a community that values honesty and transparency, they help people feel trusted and like they belong. People are more willing to participate in and give back to a community that they respect and trust, which can result in increased civic engagement and a stronger feeling of social responsibility.

In summary, developing straightforward, honest communication is crucial for creating understanding, trust, and deep connections. Honesty, simplicity, empathy, and active listening are qualities that we may prioritize to improve communication and build more satisfying relationships. These values are helpful not only in social situations but also in work and community contexts, where they foster an atmosphere that is more cooperative, courteous, and encouraging. A more authentic human experience and more profound understanding can result from adopting honesty and simplicity in a society where communication is frequently complicated and surface-level.

Cultivating Gratitude and Appreciation

A transformative practice that can significantly improve one's quality of life by promoting a sense of well-being, happiness, and interpersonal connection is cultivating gratitude and appreciation. While appreciation goes beyond recognition to include value and cherishing those significant parts of life, gratitude only entails recognizing and acknowledging those positive aspects of life. When combined, these habits can result in a life that is more purposeful and happier. People can improve their mental and emotional well-being, change their perspective, and forge deeper relationships by consciously focusing on appreciation and thankfulness.

Mindfulness, the practice of being totally present in the moment and conscious of one's thoughts, feelings, and surroundings, is the first step on the path to developing gratitude. People who practice mindfulness are better able to recognize and value the little but frequently ignored benefits in their daily lives. These might be more substantial experiences like reaching personal goals or having the support of loved ones, or they can be simpler pleasures like a stunning sunrise or a thoughtful act from a stranger. By focusing on these occasions, people might cultivate a more profound appreciation for life.

Writing in a journal is a valuable tool for developing thankfulness. Writing down one's blessings on a regular basis is the practice of keeping a gratitude journal. People are encouraged by this practice to take stock of their daily experiences and identify the good things in their lives. This can eventually assist in changing the emphasis from what is lacking or incorrect to what is plentiful and proceeding well. According to research, keeping a thankfulness notebook on a daily basis might enhance general well-being, lower stress levels, and promote happiness.

Giving thanks to others is another effective technique to foster appreciation. This can be accomplished via written letters, pleasant gestures, or vocal appreciation. When people show thankfulness, they not only reinforce their own good emotions but also help others feel valued and appreciated. Relationships can be strengthened, and a sense of belonging and community can be created via this reciprocal process. By expressing thankfulness, one may also promote a culture of appreciation and positivism, which makes everyone feel appreciated and recognized.

Savoring happy memories is another way to cultivate thankfulness. To truly savor a moment is to immerse oneself in its entirety, to enjoy it, and to mentally relive it in order to prolong the sense of gratitude and joy. This may be as easy as pausing to savor a wonderful meal, a moving song, or an insightful conversation. Through deliberate savoring of these moments, people can improve their general state of happiness and fulfillment.

Experiencing gratitude can be especially effective in redefining obstacles and struggles. When faced with hardship, concentrating on the lessons that can be learned or the modest but positive things that can be found will help develop resilience and a more positive approach. This entails weighing the good that is still present in order to balance out the pain and suffering, not to minimize or ignore it. This well-rounded viewpoint can offer consolation and fortitude when things are difficult.

As gratitude and appreciation go hand in hand, appreciation entails valuing and realizing the worth of someone or something. It necessitates a more profound recognition that extends beyond appreciating the advantages. To be appreciative is to value and be grateful for these advantages. For example, showing your friend how much you value them and their distinct qualities, as well as their contributions to your life goes a long way toward showing them how much you appreciate them.

One can cultivate gratitude for oneself as well. Acknowledging one's own accomplishments, positive traits, and strengths is a crucial aspect of self-appreciation. By doing this, you may combat negative self-talk and cultivate a more positive self-image. People can increase their confidence and sense of self-worth by appreciating and acknowledging their own work and achievements. A crucial component of mental health and self-care is self-appreciation.

There is ample evidence to support the benefits of developing appreciation and thankfulness. According to research, engaging in these activities can result in a variety of advantageous effects, such as enhanced relationships, more life satisfaction, better physical health, and increased happiness. Thankfulness and gratitude also help lessen the symptoms of anxiety and depression by drawing attention away from unfavorable ideas and emotions. They support emotional resilience and a positive outlook, which makes it easier for people to handle stress and hardship.

Developing an attitude of appreciation and thankfulness provides social and communal benefits in addition to personal ones. A culture of thankfulness in the workplace can boost staff morale, increase output, and improve collaboration. Employees are more likely to be motivated and involved in their work when they feel valued and appreciated. In a similar vein, cultivating thankfulness and appreciation within a community helps strengthen its support systems. When people feel appreciated and acknowledged, they are more likely to help and encourage one another.

Furthermore, developing an attitude of appreciation and thankfulness might raise general life satisfaction. People who develop the habit of appreciating and acknowledging the good things in their lives are more likely to feel happy and fulfilled. This technique promotes a more upbeat and cheerful view of life by encouraging an emphasis on abundance rather than lack. People who are more conscious of the chances and blessings around them may eventually experience a stronger sense of meaning and purpose as a result of this.

Finally, developing an attitude of appreciation and thankfulness is an assertive discipline that has the capacity to change a person's life. People can improve their well-being, forge closer bonds with others, and create a feeling of belonging by consciously emphasizing their strengths and appreciating the good in themselves and others. The practice of appreciation and thankfulness has several advantages, whether it is through writing, mindfulness, expressing gratitude, relishing good times, or rephrasing difficulties. It causes one to refocus attention from what is missing to what is abundant, encouraging optimism and fortitude. Embracing appreciation and thankfulness can lead to a more contented and cheerful life in a society where stress and negativity are commonplace.

Recognizing and valuing the uniqueness of relationships

Forging strong, lasting connections with other people requires an appreciation of and recognition of the unique qualities of relationships. Every connection has unique dynamics and qualities, whether it is with a spouse, friend, family member, or coworker. Our relationships can be strengthened, and the quality of our interactions can be improved by acknowledging and respecting these distinctions. We can approach relationships with more empathy, respect, and authenticity when we recognize their uniqueness.

A relationship's distinctiveness originates from the combination of the people in it as well as the environment in which it grows. The unique personalities, experiences, and viewpoints that each individual brings to the partnership influence its dynamics. The richness and diversity of relationships stem from this individuality. A friendship made later in life will not be the same as one developed in childhood, for example. An unbreakable link is formed with a childhood buddy due to their shared history and experiences that cannot be duplicated with other people. Like this, a sibling's relationship differs from a spouse's because of the unique bond formed by shared upbringing and familial bonds.

Acknowledging the distinctiveness of relationships entails realizing that every relationship fulfills a distinct function in our lives. While some relationships offer intellectual stimulation or professional collaboration, others only provide emotional support. Understanding these different responsibilities enables us to appreciate the contributions that each relationship provides to our general well-being. In the workplace, for instance, a mentor-mentee connection facilitates professional development and assistance, whereas a close friendship offers companionship and emotional support. Though they satisfy distinct needs and improve our lives in various ways, both kinds of partnerships are worthwhile.

Appreciating and appreciating the distinctiveness of relationships requires empathy. Gaining empathy entails sharing and comprehending the thoughts, emotions, and viewpoints of others. We may more fully value each other's distinct contributions to the partnership when we put ourselves in their position. Mutual respect and stronger friendships are fostered by this knowledge. For instance, having a better understanding of a partner's past experiences and how they influence their behavior might result in relationships that are more supportive and caring. In a similar vein, we can provide more resounding support and encouragement when we acknowledge the difficulties a friend may be encountering.

Recognizing and appreciating the distinctions between people is another way to honor the uniqueness of every relationship. Cultural backgrounds, individual values, communication preferences, and life experiences are a few examples of these distinctions. Our connections are enhanced, and our own perspectives are widened when we embrace this diversity instead of attempting to normalize our encounters. A friendship with someone from a different cultural background, for instance, can open our eyes to fresh perspectives and increase our comprehension of the world. We may build more varied and inclusive connections that represent the diversity of the human experience if we value these differences.

A vital component of appreciating and respecting the distinctiveness of relationships is communication. In order to communicate effectively, we must not only express ourselves clearly but also actively and attentively listen to others. For a relationship to work, various communication philosophies can be needed. Certain partnerships, for example, maybe more comfortable with infrequent but meaningful interactions, while others may thrive on open and regular communication. By adjusting our communication style to match the needs of each connection, we can ensure that our interactions are supportive and rewarding.

Acknowledging and valuing the way relationships grow and change throughout time is another way to value their uniqueness. Relationships are dynamic; they evolve and change as the people in them mature and go through different stages of life. Relationships are incredibly gratifying and fascinating because of their dynamic nature. A friend from college, for instance, may experience changes in their friendship as they advance in their personal and professional lives. It is possible to maintain the relationship's vibrancy and significance by embracing and strengthening the link in the face of these changes.

Creating and sustaining unique connections takes work and intentionality. It entails devoting time and effort to cultivating the relationship and getting to know the other person. This can involve sharing activities, having in-depth discussions, and expressing gratitude for the contributions made by the other person. To enhance emotional connection and fortify a relationship, routinely spend quality time with a partner and show thanks for their assistance. Similarly, you can preserve and strengthen a friendship by making an effort to keep up with a friend who lives far away and demonstrating interest in their life.

Beyond just making you happy, there are further advantages to appreciating and acknowledging the unique qualities of partnerships. A community that is more harmonic and cohesive can result from these behaviors. People contribute to an inclusive and empathetic culture when they recognize and value the diversity of interactions. More robust, more encouraging social networks and communities may result from this. For example, there is probably going to be more cooperation, creativity, and general job happiness in a work environment that values the distinctiveness of every professional connection. Respected and valued workers are more likely to be motivated and engaged, which enhances the atmosphere at work and produces excellent outcomes.

Furthermore, appreciating and acknowledging the unique qualities of relationships might further our own personal development. Engaging with other people and grasping their viewpoints might help us question our preconceptions and extend our perspectives. Increased self-awareness and a better comprehension of the outside environment may result from this. A friendship with someone who holds a different perspective, for example, can open our eyes to fresh perspectives and force us to consider our own values and ideas more carefully. Our lives are enhanced by this process of reciprocal learning and development, which also broadens our horizons and increases our empathy.

In summary, developing strong, meaningful connections and advancing a sense of community and understanding depends on appreciating and respecting the uniqueness of interactions. We can approach relationships with more empathy, respect, and authenticity if we recognize their uniqueness. Building and sustaining these unique connections requires deliberate effort, empathy, and effective communication. Beyond just enhancing one's own happiness, this activity also strengthens and supports communities and social networks. Respecting the individuality of relationships improves our lives and deepens our understanding of the human condition in a multicultural and globally interconnected world.

Celebrating small, imperfect moments together

It can significantly improve our lives and relationships to practice celebrating little, imperfect moments with one another. Discovering happiness and significance in the commonplace, flawed moments can bring a sense of contentment and connection in a society that frequently places a premium on perfection and enormous accomplishments. Even though they may not seem like much, these experiences have the power to strengthen our relationships with one another and produce enduring memories.

The idea of mindfulness lies at the core of appreciating the little, imperfect moments in life. Being mindful is focusing all of one's attention on the here and now and accepting it as it is without passing judgment. By doing this, we become more aware of and appreciative of life's little pleasures, which we may otherwise take for granted. When done mindfully, activities like having coffee with a loved one, taking a stroll in the park, or sharing a good laugh over a minor incident may all lead to great joy. These moments don't have to be remarkable or flawless to be valuable; in fact, their flaws frequently make them more endearing and genuine.

A crucial component of appreciating these occasions is accepting imperfection. Because life is intrinsically imperfect, aiming for perfection can cause needless anxiety and disillusionment. We invite a more genuine and satisfying experience into our lives when we embrace our flaws and even celebrate them. A family get-together, for instance, can still be lovely and unforgettable even if the food is a little overdone or the décor isn't perfect. What matters most are the interactions, laughs, and conversations that take place. We can relate to these experiences more deeply because of their human and understandable flaws.

Appreciating the little, flawed things in life also helps you feel grateful. By taking the time to be thankful for the small things in life, we can develop an attitude of thankfulness that can improve our general well-being. Our attention is redirected from what is lacking in our lives to what is rich and present when we are grateful. It enables us to cherish the people and things that make us happy and to take delight in the little things in life. For example, thanking your partner for tiny gestures of kindness, like making breakfast or leaving a lovely note, can improve the relationship and foster an environment of appreciation.

Celebrating these occasions with your partner can build a solid foundation of memories and shared experiences. Small, routine exchanges are frequently what create and maintain connections over time. Connecting and bonding can occur through simple things like cooking together, watching a favorite movie, or going for a walk. People can converse, spend quality time together, and express their views and feelings through these activities. Failed recipes and unexpected downpours are examples of imperfect events that can bring comedy and resiliency to a relationship, strengthening the bonds between people and encouraging cooperation.

Furthermore, savoring the little, imperfect moments in life can strengthen our fortitude and improve our capacity to handle hardship. Unpredictability characterizes life, and things rarely happen as planned. We cultivate a more adaptable and flexible mindset when we discover happiness and purpose in the midst of imperfect circumstances. Because of our resilience, we can overcome adversity with a positive outlook and look for the bright side of adverse circumstances. An annoyance can become a treasured memory, for example, by using a power outage to host a game night or a romantic meal. These encounters teach us to appreciate the little things in life and to find happiness in the unexpected.

Celebrating the little, imperfect moments in family life can foster a loving and encouraging atmosphere. Particularly young children gain from witnessing their parents accept flaws and take pleasure in leisurely pursuits. It imparts to kids essential knowledge about relationships, thankfulness, and resilience. A feeling of security and belonging can be fostered by family customs like impromptu dance parties in the living room or weekly game nights. These customs are valuable because they encourage shared love, laughter, and connections; they don't have to be complex or flawlessly carried out.

Celebrating the little, imperfect moments in friendships can strengthen the relationship and foster a sense of unity. Friends who can find humor in each other's small disasters, like getting lost on a road trip or trying a do-it-yourself project that goes wrong, tend to be stronger and more resilient than other friends. Because of these shared experiences, friends grow to support and enjoy one another's company no matter what happens. This fosters trust and understanding. Together, being able to embrace each other's flaws helps promote a more genuine and long-lasting connection.

There are effects on our mental health from appreciating the little, imperfect moments in life. Stress, worry, and burnout can result from the pressure to always aim higher and attain perfection. This pressure can be lessened, and a more balanced and satisfying existence can be created by concentrating on the little, ordinary moments and accepting their flaws. It enables us to enjoy the journey rather than just the destination and to appreciate the present. Having this mentality can increase one's level of contentment in life in general.

Small, imperfect moments should be acknowledged and celebrated at work in order to foster a supportive and upbeat work environment. Little acts of kindness, like praising a coworker's work, commemorating a small team's accomplishment, or pausing to share a joke, can lift spirits and create a feeling of community. These are the kinds of moments that are valuable because they are genuine and spontaneous, not because they have to be flawless or well-orchestrated. Organizations can foster a culture where employees feel valued and inspired by appreciating these connections.

In conclusion, it is a discipline that can improve our lives and relationships to share in little, imperfect moments with one another. We may discover happiness and purpose in the commonplace moments that comprise our lives by accepting attentiveness, thankfulness, and the beauty of imperfections. Even though they may not seem like much, these experiences have the power to strengthen our bonds with one another and produce enduring memories. Celebrating these occasions, whether they are in the setting of a relationship, family, or office, promotes resilience, well-being, and a feeling of community. Finding joy in the small, imperfect moments enables us to live more truthfully and to see the depth of our human experience in a world that frequently stresses perfection and big successes.

CHAPTER V

Personal Growth and Self-Acceptance

Self-compassion and self-forgiveness

Essential components of emotional health and personal development are self-compassion and self-forgiveness. They entail loving ourselves, acknowledging and embracing our flaws, and moving past our errors with comprehension and forgiveness. Adopting these habits can result in a life that is more robust, balanced, and satisfying.

The act of showing kindness and understanding to oneself when experiencing pain or feeling inadequate is known as self-compassion. It entails accepting our own suffering and difficulties without passing judgment and realizing that everyone experiences imperfection. Commonly, self-compassion is separated into three parts: mindfulness, common humanity, and self-kindness. Treating oneself with the same consideration and compassion that one would provide a friend is the essence of self-kindness. The knowledge that everyone faces challenges and errs is known as common humanity. Being mindful is allowing our emotions to be there without overidentifying with them or repressing them.

Emotional resilience can be significantly improved by engaging in self-compassionate practices. We strengthen our capacity to handle stress and hardship when we respond to our own suffering with kindness as opposed to self-criticism. When we are self-compassionate, we are able to face the difficulties of life with warmth and support instead of being critical and harsh with ourselves. This change in viewpoint can improve mental health by lowering anxiety and depressive symptoms. For example, when we experience rejection or failure, self-compassion helps us to remember that failure is a regular aspect of learning and progress rather than criticizing ourselves for not being perfect.

Conversely, self-forgiveness entails letting go of self-directed resentment or shame for previous transgressions or errors. It's about owning up to our mistakes, accepting responsibility, trying to make reparations, and then letting go of the guilt. Self-forgiveness is about releasing ourselves from the bad feelings that can impede our happiness and personal development, not about accepting responsibility for our faults. We may move forward with self-acceptance and serenity thanks to this practice.

Accepting responsibility for our acts is often the first step in the self-forgiveness process. This entails being open about our errors and cognizant of the potential effects they may have had on both others and ourselves. Accepting responsibility is an essential first step because it creates the space for sincere regret and the desire to set things right. But it's also critical to strike a balance between this obligation and self-compassion and understanding. To be able to forgive oneself, we must first acknowledge that everyone makes mistakes and that these faults do not determine our value.

Finding a way to make amends is another crucial component of self-forgiveness. This may entail expressing regret to the people we have offended, making amends, or figuring out how to make things right. Making apologies promotes closure and healing by mending relationships and restoring trust. But it's also critical to recognize that not every circumstance can be changed, and in certain circumstances, learning how to forgive oneself on the inside becomes more vital.

The hardest part of self-forgiveness is usually letting go of the guilt on oneself. It entails turning our attention from previous transgressions to the here and now and beyond. Self-compassion and mindfulness practices can help this process along. Being mindful enables us to remain in the now and impartially examine our ideas and feelings. The emotional support required to let go of self-blame and to treat ourselves with kindness and understanding comes from having self-compassion.

Self-forgiveness and self-compassion are closely related and reinforce one another. Self-compassion cultivates an atmosphere of love and understanding within oneself, which facilitates self-forgiveness. In a similar vein, self-forgiveness fosters self-compassion by enabling us to get past our errors and care for ourselves in the same compassionate and understanding ways that we would others. When combined, these techniques help us develop emotional fortitude and self-acceptance, which makes it easier and more graceful for us to deal with life's obstacles.

Beyond just improving our own well-being, self-compassion and self-forgiveness also strengthen our bonds with others. We are more inclined to treat other people with compassion and forgiveness when we practice these qualities toward ourselves. As we become less critical of others and more accepting of their flaws and shortcomings, this might result in more sympathetic and encouraging interactions. Furthermore, letting go of our emotional baggage and practicing self-compassion and self-forgiveness can help us be more present and approachable in our relationships with others.

In the context of personal development, cultivating a growth mindset requires self-compassion and self-forgiveness. Having a growth mindset means not seeing obstacles and failures as signs of inadequacy or failure but rather as chances for learning and development. Self-forgiveness enables us to go forward without being constrained by our mistakes from the past, while self-compassion gives us the emotional security required to take chances and learn from them. When combined, these procedures foster a climate within the company that is conducive to ongoing learning and development.

Our feeling of general meaning and purpose in life can also be improved by practicing self-compassion and self-forgiveness. We are more likely to pursue our objectives and passions with drive and confidence when we are kind and understanding to ourselves. Self-forgiveness allows us to let go of the past and concentrate on what really matters to us, while self-compassion helps us remain resilient in the face of failures. A life that is more meaningful and rewarding can be facilitated by having a clear purpose and direction.

In conclusion, we can change our relationships with others and ourselves by practicing self-compassion and self-forgiveness. We may improve our mental health, strengthen our resilience, and promote a growth mindset by accepting our flaws and being kind to ourselves. Self-forgiveness releases us from the weight of self-blame and enables us to move past our errors and concentrate on the here and now and the future. When combined, these techniques foster an environment that is constructive and encourages personal development, deep connections, and a happy existence. Accepting self-compassion and self-forgiveness is a constant process that calls for perseverance, repetition, and dedication. The path does, however, have significant benefits, including increased emotional resilience, self-acceptance, and general well-being.

Overcoming the fear of failure

A critical first step toward achieving both professional and personal progress is overcoming the fear of failure. People might get paralyzed by this widespread dread, which keeps them from realizing their full potential and achieving their aspirations. Understanding the causes of this fear, altering our perspective, and creating plans to boost confidence and resilience are all necessary for addressing and managing it.

A person's fear of failing can have many different origins, such as personal experiences, upbringing, and societal expectations. Many people are socialized from an early age to believe that success proves their value, and that failure is a sign of personal inferiority. Social standards that stigmatize mistakes and applaud accomplishments serve to foster this way of thinking. As a result, people could have a deep-rooted dread of failing, which would limit their willingness to attempt new things and take chances. For instance, a student who gets negative feedback on their grade could grow afraid of failing in other aspects of their life and pass up chances for learning and personal development.

Overcoming this anxiety requires a shift in how we view failure. We can reframe failure as a great learning experience instead of seeing it as a bad thing. This change in viewpoint entails realizing that failure is a necessary step on the path to achievement and personal development. Every setback offers the chance to learn new things, acquire new abilities, and strengthen resilience. For example, a lot of prosperous businesspeople and inventors have gone through several setbacks prior to making their breakthroughs. We can lessen failure's paralyzing effect and increase our willingness to take chances by accepting it as a normal and productive part of the process.

One effective strategy for getting over the fear of failing is to adopt a growth mentality. A growth mindset, as defined by psychologist Carol Dweck, is the conviction that our skills and intelligence can be enhanced by commitment and diligence. This is in opposition to a fixed worldview, which maintains that our capacities are fixed and unalterable. Having a growth mindset helps us to see obstacles and failures as chances for improvement rather than as dangers to our value as individuals. An athlete who has a growth mentality, for instance, will view a subpar performance as an opportunity to pinpoint areas for growth and to put in more effort rather than as proof that they are incapable of succeeding.

Another essential component of conquering the fear of failing is developing resilience. The capacity to overcome adversity and continue on one's path is known as resilience. Practicing self-compassion, having a positive outlook, and adopting stress management techniques are all part of building resilience. We can better manage the emotional effects of failure and keep our motivation and confidence by building our resilience. For example, instead of giving up on their dream, a writer who receives rejection from publications might use resilience to keep improving their work and sending it to new prospects.

Reducing the fear of failing can also be accomplished by setting reasonable and attainable goals. Setting and achieving achievable objectives gives us a sense of accomplishment and development that can increase our self-esteem and lessen our fear of failing. The process can be made less intimidating and more doable by breaking down more significant objectives into more minor, more achievable phases. To make the eventual objective more feasible and practical, one could create progressive targets, like finishing a 5k race and then gradually increasing the distance, rather than aiming to complete a marathon without any prior training.

Getting assistance from others is yet another crucial tactic for conquering the fear of failing. Gaining perspective, support, and guidance from mentors, family members, or trustworthy friends when we share our worries and difficulties with them can be pretty beneficial. We can feel more emboldened to take chances and less alone in our problems when we have supportive relationships. For instance, a mentor who has successfully overcome comparable obstacles can offer advice and support to an entrepreneur who is afraid to start a new company. By creating a support system, we can acquire the self-assurance and drive required to face our anxieties and strive toward our objectives.

Self-compassion exercises are essential for controlling the fear of failing. When we encounter challenges, self-compassion entails being gentle and patient with ourselves instead of being unduly harsh and critical. We can lessen the negative self-talk that frequently accompanies the dread of failure by accepting our flaws and the fact that failure is a common human experience. For instance, a student who does not pass an exam can demonstrate self-compassion by telling themselves that one failure does not define who they are or what they are capable of and by making positive changes to their performance going forward.

Becoming aware of oneself and practicing stress reduction are essential steps towards conquering the fear of failing. Being mindful entails giving your whole attention to the here and now without passing judgment. By increasing our awareness of our thoughts and emotions, this exercise can help us better control them. Stress-reduction methods, including deep breathing, meditation, and training, can enhance our general well-being and lessen the anxiety brought on by the dread of failing. A professional facing a high-stakes presentation, for example, can utilize stress management and mindfulness strategies to remain composed and focused, which lowers the anxiety of making mistakes.

Ultimately, one of the best strategies to get over our fear of failing is to act in spite of our worries. We develop courage and resilience when we confront our concerns head-on and leave our comfort zones. Even if a modest step toward our goals is fraught with risk and uncertainty, everyone counts toward lessening the influence of our concerns. A budding artist who is afraid of receiving negative feedback from the public, for instance, can begin by showing their work to a small, encouraging group before gaining the confidence to present it to a larger audience. By repeatedly putting ourselves in fear-inducing circumstances, we can gain the trust and sense of mastery that allows us to go after our dreams.

To sum up, overcoming the fear of failing is a complex process that includes adopting a different perspective, strengthening our resilience, establishing reasonable goals, getting help, engaging in self-compassion exercises, and acting on our anxieties. We can reframe failure as a worthwhile learning experience and build the self-assurance and drive required to pursue our goals by comprehending and resolving the causes of our fear. Accepting failure as a necessary component of the path to achievement and personal development enables us to live more fully and truthfully, realizing our potential and realizing our aspirations.

Growth through Simplicity

A philosophy known as "growth through simplicity" highlights the importance of leading a simple life that is centered on the things that are really important. Amidst a time marked by swift technological progress and an unceasing flood of data, the notion of simplicity offers a novel and profound strategy for individual and community development. This section examines the many facets of growth via simplicity, including relationships, productivity, mental and emotional health, and general life satisfaction.

Simplifying essentially means cutting out the extras and concentrating on what matters most. This method can be used in many areas of life, including our everyday routines, mental spaces, and physical surroundings. We make room for the things that genuinely improve our lives by getting rid of things and distractions that aren't really important. Decluttering involves more than just getting rid of stuff; it also consists in streamlining our responsibilities, relationships, and ideas. It's about putting depth over breadth and quality above quantity.

The favorable effect that adopting simplicity has on mental and emotional health is among its most important advantages. A road to inner peace and fulfillment can be found in simplicity, even in a society that frequently exalts busyness and financial achievement. The mental congestion that results from juggling an excessive number of responsibilities, belongings, and social obligations is diminished when we simplify our lives. Because there is less mental clutter, we can concentrate more intently on the here and now, which promotes mindfulness and lowers stress. Research has demonstrated that mindfulness techniques, which are strongly related to simple principles, can result in enhanced emotional resilience, better mental health, and increased happiness all around.

Additionally, simplicity promotes a closer relationship with oneself. We may more easily tune into our own wants, desires, and values when we remove the noise and distractions of modern life. Being self-aware is essential for personal development because it enables us to make choices that are in line with our genuine selves rather than those dictated by other people or society. Greater contentment and a sense of purpose, for instance, can result from deciding to follow a career that is in line with our inclinations rather than one that is traditionally prestigious. In a similar vein, we can feel more connected and like we belong when we streamline our social lives and concentrate on relationships that are genuinely meaningful.

Simplicity in relationships encourages depth and genuineness. We make room for more sincere and profound connections when we value meaningful interactions over fleeting social interactions. Simplifying our relationships means putting more of our resources into the ones that provide happiness, progress, and support while letting go of the poisonous or draining ones. Bonds that are stronger and more resilient might result from this deliberate approach to relationships. For example, concentrating on a small number of close friendships enables more meaningful and encouraging encounters than overcommitting to many casual acquaintances. These close relationships offer shared experiences, helpful criticism, and emotional support, all of which lay a strong foundation for personal development.

The idea of simplicity also encompasses how we approach productivity and labor. A different route to reaching our objectives is provided by simplicity in a society that frequently confuses busyness with achievement. We can become more productive and efficient by narrowing our attention to what is really important and getting rid of things that aren't necessary. This method, also known as essentialism, entails deciding which chores and projects are most essential to do first and letting go of the rest. Essentialism enables us to focus our efforts and resources on the things that will make the most difference, resulting in more noteworthy and satisfying accomplishments. Instead of balancing several projects, a writer may, for instance, concentrate on honing a single book, producing a higher caliber and more significant piece of work.

Additionally, simplicity fosters a more positive relationship with material belongings. In a culture that prioritizes consumption, we are frequently taught that acquiring more possessions will make us happier and more successful. However, studies have shown that material belongings do not really improve our well-being after a certain point. Instead, they might end up being a cause of anxiety and diversion. We can liberate ourselves from the weight of unnecessary belongings and make room for experiences and pursuits that genuinely fulfill us by embracing simplicity and adopting minimalism. This may be clearing out the clutter from our houses, buying with greater intention, and placing a higher value on experiences than material possessions. For example, rather than spending money on the newest technology, we can decide to fund an enjoyable vacation or a fulfilling pastime.

Our physical health benefits from living simply as well. Healthy behaviors like eating whole foods, exercising frequently, and getting enough sleep are all part of a simpler lifestyle. Prioritizing our health and well-being makes it easier for us to achieve our objectives and overcome obstacles in life. Furthermore, more straightforward nutrition and exercise regimens that emphasize fundamentals above fads or intense training can have a longer-lasting positive impact on health.

Additionally, simplicity can strengthen our sense of fulfillment and purpose. We are more inclined to partake in activities that are consistent with our values and passions when we eliminate extravagance and concentrate on what really matters. Our everyday lives become more meaningful and satisfying as a result of this congruence. A person who values creativity, for instance, can find more happiness and pleasure in making time for their art than in juggling a busy schedule full of commitments that don't align with their moral principles. This emphasis on worthwhile endeavors helps us grow ourselves and enables us to positively influence the environment.

Simplicity also encourages a more conscious and sustainable way of living. We can improve our planet's health by cutting back on our trash and consumption. Simplicity's environmental benefits are consistent with the more general objectives of conservation and sustainability. Living simply makes us more conscious of our resources and deliberate in our decisions, which promotes a more harmonious and balanced relationship with the environment. This could entail taking up habits like cutting back on trash, saving energy, and promoting sustainable goods and services.

To sum up, growth via simplicity is a complex strategy that has the potential to significantly improve a number of facets of our lives. We make room for deeper connections, meaningful production, mental and emotional well-being, and general life happiness by concentrating on what really matters and getting rid of the excess. Adopting a simple lifestyle promotes a sense of authenticity and fulfillment by helping us connect with others and ourselves on a deeper level. It urges us to live more sustainably and in accordance with our beliefs and passions. It also supports a healthier lifestyle. The road to more serenity, meaning, and personal development is simplicity in an often confusing and stressful environment.

Prioritizing what truly matters

Setting priorities for what really counts is a crucial notion that helps people live more purposeful and fulfilling lives. The capacity to recognize and concentrate on what matters most can result in increased clarity, fulfillment, and personal development in a society full of incessant distractions, conflicting expectations, and social pressures.

Prioritization is fundamentally about choosing carefully where to spend our time, effort, and money. It calls on us to recognize our beliefs, objectives, and aspirations and to direct our behavior in accordance with them. Setting priorities involves more than just organizing our workload effectively; it also involves choosing choices deliberately that correspond to our core values and goals. A person who prioritizes family relationships, for instance, could put spending time with loved ones above advancing in their job or accumulating material goods.

One of the primary benefits of prioritizing what actually matters is the development of overall well-being. When we focus on activities and relationships that correspond with our values and provide us joy and fulfillment, we enjoy greater satisfaction in our daily lives. Living true to who we are instead of fitting in with social norms or expectations from other sources brings us this sense of fulfillment. For instance, someone who prioritizes creativity and self-expression may find enormous happiness in pursuing artistic undertakings, even if they do not lead to financial success or notoriety.

Setting priorities promotes focus and clarity as well. We can reduce or get rid of distractions that take us away from our objectives by determining what our top priorities are. This clarity allows us to manage our time and resources more effectively, boosting our productivity and lowering feelings of overload. A professional who places a high priority on career development, for instance, might establish precise objectives and timelines, which enables them to use their time and energy wisely.

Moreover, focusing on what is genuinely essential fosters personal growth and development. Investing in challenging and values-aligned activities opens us up to new possibilities for learning, growth, and development. This ongoing evolution not only strengthens our talents but also enriches our lives with fresh experiences and views. An individual who places a high priority on their health and well-being, for example, may exercise frequently and adopt a nutritious diet, which would enhance their physical fitness and general well-being.

In relationships, priority deepens bonds and promotes deeper connections. We develop intimacy, trust, and support from one another when we put time and effort into meaningful relationships. Active listening, empathy, and placing a high value on spending quality time together are all part of this purposeful approach to relationships. A parent who places a high priority on fostering their child's emotional growth, for instance, might have frequent chats, offer emotional support, and take part in activities that deepen their relationship.

Setting priorities also promotes a more balanced and sustainable way of living. Setting priorities enables us to set boundaries and make wise decisions about how we spend our time and energy in a society that frequently values activity and production over well-being. Reducing stress, avoiding burnout, and preserving general health all depend on this balance. A person who values work-life balance, for instance, could schedule leisure, hobbies, and self-care activities to make sure they have the stamina and fortitude to successfully pursue their objectives.

Saying no to obligations or activities that conflict with our priorities is another essential skill for effective prioritization. To stay focused and succeed over the long run, we must be able to set limits and make decisions based on our beliefs and objectives. Saying no can be difficult, particularly in a society that prizes production and bustle, but it's necessary to save our time and energy for the things that really count. One way to prioritize activities that support our personal growth and well-being is to decline social invitations and professional initiatives that don't correspond with our priorities.

In conclusion, one effective method for leading a more purposeful and happy life is to prioritize the things that are really important. We can improve our general well-being, encourage personal development, fortify relationships, and attain more clarity and focus by defining our values, goals, and aspirations and deliberately choosing how to spend our time and energy. Setting priorities frees us from the influence of societal norms or other forces to live honestly and genuinely as our actual selves. Prioritization is a guiding concept that we can use to create a balanced, meaningful lifestyle that is consistent with our highest goals and beliefs.

CONCLUSION

Ultimately, "Embracing Wabi-Sabi: Finding Beauty in Imperfection and Simplicity" presents a profoundly transformational viewpoint on our understanding of and interactions with the world. The book invites readers to let go of the unrelenting quest for perfection and instead discover calm and beauty in the imperfect and transient through its incisive analysis of the Wabi-Sabi philosophy. We can develop a greater sense of peace and harmony by accepting the cycles of growth and decay that are a part of life's natural rhythm.

This book's practical Wabi-Sabi applications offer a way to incorporate this ageless concept into our everyday existence. Wabi-Sabi can help us live more honestly and appreciatively through the simplification of our surroundings, the cultivation of genuine connections, and the adoption of a more attentive attitude to daily activities. The author gives readers the tools to change their perspective and way of life by teaching them how to be grateful, mindful, and accepting of life's flaws.

In the end, "Embracing Wabi-Sabi" is an appeal to get back to the fundamentals, to enjoy simplicity, and to see the beauty in the transient and flawed. Readers are asked to set out on a path toward a more peaceful, meaningful, and fulfilling life by internalizing the precepts of Wabi-Sabi. This book is a gentle reminder that the simple and fleeting moments that we often ignore are where true beauty and fulfillment may usually be found rather than the perfect and enduring.

Thank you for buying and reading/ listening to our book. If you found this book useful/ helpful please take a few minutes and leave a review on the platform where you purchased our book. Your feedback matters greatly to us.

www.ingramcontent.com/pod-product-compliance
Lightning Source LLC
Chambersburg PA
CBHW072014150726
47999CB00002B/657